The
Angel of Ashland

The
Angel of Ashland

*Practicing Compassion
and Tempting Fate*

A BIOGRAPHY OF
ROBERT SPENCER, M.D.

Vincent J. Genovese

Prometheus Books
59 John Glenn Drive
Amherst, New York 14228-2197

Published 2000 by Prometheus Books

Inquiries should be addressed to
Prometheus Books
59 John Glenn Drive
Amherst, New York 14228–2197
VOICE: 716–691–0133, ext. 207
FAX: 716–564–2711
WWW.PROMETHEUSBOOKS.COM

04 03 02 01 00   5 4 3 2 1

Library of Congress Cataloging-in-Publication Data

Genovese, Vincent J., 1945–
    The angel of Ashland : practicing compassion and tempting fate / Vincent J. Genovese.
        p. cm.
    Includes index.
    ISBN 1–57392–831–3 (alk. paper)
    1. Spencer, Robert Douglas, 1889–1969. 2. Physicians—Pennsylvania—Biography. 3. Abortion—Pennsylvania—History. I. Title.

R154.S676 G46 2000
610'.9'2—dc21
[B]   00–055263

Printed in the United States of America on acid-free paper

CONTENTS

ACKNOWLEDGMENTS

The support of many people, organizations, and publications was instrumental in the completion of this work. I am indebted to the following: Eleanor Becker Spencer, Steve Sukunda, Paul Reidler, Atty. Harry Strouse of Strouse and Strouse, American Medical Association, Pennsylvania State University, Schuykill County Court Records, Association for the Study of Abortions, Lulu Anns, Mrs. Wally Sears, Melanie Wade, and Ed Conrad.

Eleanor B. Spencer, the widow of Dr. Robert B. Spencer, created a fund, in memory of her husband, to provide scholarships to area high school graduates. Contributions to the fund should be sent to: Schuylkill Area Community Foundation, 816 Center Street, Ashland, PA 17921.

INTRODUCTION

I would be the first one to admit that as I sat watching television one evening in late January of 1969, I had never heard of Dr. Robert Douglas Spencer. The *Huntley-Brinkley Report* was preparing to come on. It was a show that I began viewing faithfully while a college student at West Chester University and to which I was now somewhat addicted. Much to my surprise the lead story struck very close to home. Chet Huntley broke the news with the statement that Dr. Robert Spencer, also known as the "Angel of Ashland," had died. Huntley went on to describe how this "King of the Abortionists" had performed 100,000 abortions during his medical career, which spanned over half a century from the 1920s to that day. All this occurred in the sleepy little coalmining town of Ashland, Pennsylvania.

I was born and raised by a coal-miner father in a similar mining town not more than ten miles from Ashland. Yet, the name of Dr. Spencer meant nothing to me. Mesmerized, I soaked up every detail from the report like a sponge. Fascinated by this local player who made the lead story on the national news, I began a quest to find out more. The search, although arduous at times, was one of the most enjoyable experiences of my life and it has culminated in this book.

In writing this work I have made every effort to be factual and accurate. Unfortunately all of the major principals are now dead. Memories of the locals tend to get muddled and exaggerated over time. All the details in this volume are based on interviews with Mrs. Spencer and Mr. Steve Sukunda who was Dr. Spencer's life-long friend and assistant at the clinic they ran together. In addition, I have made a personal investigation of the doctor's private study; reviewed legal documents such as court proceedings; conducted interviews with jurors; searched reputable periodicals such as the *New York Times*, *Los Angeles Times*, *Newsweek*, and *Time*; and listened to eyewitness accounts by first-party participants. I stand by what is written here. Wherever supposition enters in, it will be so identified. The opening scene is a detailed account of the typical treatment of one of Dr. Spencer's abortion patients at the Spencer Clinic as given to me by Mr. Sukunda.

Chapter 1

DESTINATION ASHLAND, PA.

With many thanks to a fine doctor and a great humanitarian.
—former patient

Dr. Robert D. Spencer stood at the scrub sink in his eleven-room clinic located in the 500 block of Center Street in the town of Ashland in the hard-coal region of Pennsylvania. He was washing his hands before beginning the illegal abortion he was about to perform. It was the early 1960s. What a stupid, hypocritical, goddamned law, he must have thought to himself with resentment as he considered the outmoded Pennsylvania abortion law that he was about to break for the sixty-thousandth time.

Dr. Spencer finished scrubbing and put on a pair of surgical gloves as he went into the operating room to tend to his patient. Spencer had never met the nineteen-year-old woman before the prior evening. He knew only that she had come from Michigan and she needed his help. That was all he required. He had helped thousands of women like her before. They sought him out from every state in the Union and from foreign countries as well. There was no better doctor in the country, and perhaps the world, than Dr. Spencer when it came to performing an abortion.

When the young woman came to the clinic the night before, he examined her, recorded her medical history, and then treated her internally with a pastelike solution that he had invented himself.

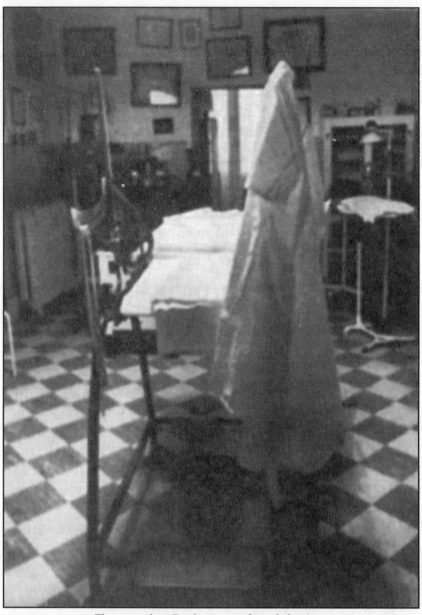

The room where Dr. Spencer performed abortions.
(Courtesy Bernard Gotfryd)

(The knowledge of the contents of this invention died with the doctor.) It would dilate the uterus while reducing the possibility of bleeding. As he entered the room, she was lying on her back on the table, naked from the waist down. Dr. Spencer moved her gently until her buttocks were at the very edge of the table. He then spread her legs apart and strapped her feet into the stirrups extending out on each side of the table. This is called the "Lithotomy Position." Understandably, being in this position makes most patients feel vulnerable. The apprehension showed in her eyes. He could tell she wanted to speak. Nervously she asked him how long it would take.

"Oh, probably only about twenty-five to thirty minutes," he would answer. Then he usually added, "Just try and relax. I promise you won't feel any pain."

Spencer possessed an angelic-looking face and said the words so convincingly that she responded almost as if under hypnosis, relaxing her taut body. He then inserted a rubber tube into her urethra.

"If you have to pass any urine, please do so now so that we don't have any accidents," he would instruct.

She obeyed and emptied her bladder. It made such an audible noise as it traveled down the tube that she was visibly embarrassed. With his back to her, Spencer completely ignored the scene by feigning business at the instrument tray. When she finished he removed both the tube and the sac. The next step was to prepare her for surgery by washing down the entire vaginal area both inside and out with gauze pads soaked in an antiseptic solution. The readily available and equally effective hexachlorophene was used.

Now she was ready. He would tell her to relax her arm and close her eyes as he informed her that he was going to give her a sedative. A shot of hexaborbital was administered intravenously and in seconds the sights and sounds around her would fade. When she was unconscious, Dr. Spencer would pull off his gloves and dispose of them.

"Another set of gloves," he would instruct his male assistant, Steve Sukunda. Steve had anticipated and was ready with a fresh set. The doctor always took this extra precaution to avoid infection. Mistakes under circumstances such as these could be costly, considering the illegality of what he was about to do. He sat on a small stool at the end of the table and adjusted the lamp on his head.

"Retractors," he called to Steve. Steve handed him two L-shaped metal devices with his gloved hands. The doctor inserted these into the patient's vagina; one on each side. With these he stretched the opening until he could clearly see the cervix.

"Tenaculum," he ordered. Steve handed him a sinister-looking instrument that closely resembles a pair of ice tongs and are almost as sharp. With this he grasped the upper lip of the cervix, gently pulling down on it.

"Number One Helgar," he would call for next. The doctor put this long metal dilator lubricated with a jellylike substance into the cervix and pulled it out. He asked for several more of these, each bigger than the one before, until he created a large enough opening at the entrance to the uterus to satisfy his needs. Spencer worked deliberately since he knew only too well how easily the cervix could be punctured. Ten minutes had gone by since he began working on her.

With the dilation complete, the next step, in what Dr. Spencer always referred to in his medical records as a D and C, was to extract the fetus. At this point most doctors prefer to use a blunt instrument called a *curette* to accomplish this. Dr. Spencer preferred using his index finger. His hands were small and extremely tuned to the touch of a uterus. Using this method greatly reduced the possibility of internal damage and bleeding. He simply inserted his finger and moved it deftly against the uterine wall, causing both fetus and placenta to break free. When he felt this happen he would call for a small pair of forceps and gently remove the seven-week-old embryo. It was discarded without any sense of loss into a basin which already held two others from this morning's work. He went back in to make sure all the products of conception were removed and that the uterus had begun to contract in order that there be no bleeding.

"She's in good shape," he announced to Steve. Doc and Steve lifted her off the table and placed her on a litter. They carried her to a recovery room down the hall from the operating room. It was now precisely thirty-one minutes from the time she was given the shot and she was beginning to come out of it. Dr. Spencer sat with her until he could see her eyes focusing clearly on him.

"How do you feel?" he would ask.

"All right," she managed.

Spencer prepared an injection of several hundred thousand units of penicillin and gave it to her.

"When you feel capable you can put your clothes back on," he said, then left her alone.

By the time she was almost fully dressed, the doctor came back. He gave her a feminine pad to put on just in case she had some mild bleeding. This embarrassed her but he was gone so quickly that the thought did not last long.

Her thoughts almost certainly turned to how she could now return to college, free from the impossible situation that her pregnancy had put her in. No more fretful sleeping at night. No more waking in the morning to the realization that an unwanted baby was a day older and further developed.

Hours later and fully dressed she waited for the doctor's return. She didn't have to wait long. Dr. Spencer spoke gently but quickly for there were others waiting.

"Here are some pills to dry up the milk in your breasts. This is a prescription for birth control pills if you want them. If you experience any heavy bleeding, see a doctor at once. But if you take it easy for about two days you should be fine."

(Few inventions can lay claim to the controversy which surrounded the introduction of the birth control pill. Contraceptive devices prior to the 1950s were mostly herbal remedies handed down through the centuries. Gregory Pincus, aided in part by a $15,000 grant from feminist Margaret Sanger, produced the first pill for sale in 1960 when he developed norethynordel. For roughly the last decade of his life Dr. Spencer was able to offer his female patients something other than condoms or the rhythm method to control their fertility. Contraceptive counseling was something he engaged in faithfully with any woman who came to him and was willing to listen.)

She took the items and stored them in her purse. Then she asked the question he'd heard so many times before.

"How much do I owe you?"

"Fifty dollars."

She opened her purse and counted out five tens, all the time thanking him profusely. One minute later she was back on the main avenue of town heading up Center Street to Weyman's Restaurant where she could catch a bus that would eventually take her back to Michigan. Dr. Spencer would never see her again. She was now relegated to number sixty thousand in his journal. There would be forty thousand more before his practice would end.

Chapter 2

THE EARLY YEARS
AND THE FORMATION
OF A PHILOSOPHY

Listen my friends and you shall hear
Of the Angel of Ashland who knew no fear.
To some he was a God send,
To others a sinner.
But throughout his long life
He was always a winner.
Each day he would walk down the main street of town.
A beret on his head that belied him a clown.
But make no mistake, this man was no fool
As he practiced his trade and broke the big rule.
He gave life to many
And brought death to others.
Thousands of babies denied sisters and brothers.

—Vincent J. Genovese

The unique story of the life and times of Dr. Robert Douglas Spencer began many years and hundreds of miles from the small Pennsylvania coal-mining town where he established his practice. Robert Spencer was born on March 16, 1889, in Kansas City, Missouri. He was the son of attorney William Spencer and his schoolteacher wife, Emily Butler Spencer. Robert's father was a conservative, soft-spoken man who practiced the Methodist faith. His mother was a sociable, talkative woman always fashionably attired and somewhat the opposite of her husband. Although a lawyer, he avoided too much interaction with people while his wife eagerly sought it out.

When Robert was two years old, the family, which included an older brother by two years, moved to the Lycoming County city of Williamsport, Pennsylvania. Here his mother stopped teaching to raise her two sons while his father practiced general law. The law practice was successful, allowing the Spencers to enjoy a nice, upper-class lifestyle.

Williamsport is located in north central Pennsylvania about one hour's drive from Pennsylvania State University. It is most often remembered as the birthplace of Little League Baseball and the home of the Little League World Series. Straddling the wide Susquehanna River with native forests covering its rolling mountains, the area near the city was the lumber capital of the country. A six-mile-long log boom stretching from shore to shore was constantly moving down the Susquehanna to market at Chesapeake Bay. Williamsport boasted the largest number of millionaires per capita in the United States. Even today the high school's nickname is "The Millionaires."

Amidst this setting, young Robert spent a carefree, happy boyhood. He loved the outdoors and roamed the length and breadth of the river and its surrounding mountains, rarely missing a chance to hunt, fish, and camp in the natural beauty around him. His father had a boat that allowed Robert the freedom to traverse the entire area with his two friends, John Hess and Roy Duck. Through their efforts, these friends formed what became one of the first Boy Scout troops in Pennsylvania.

During his entire boyhood, there were only two incidents that Robert told his second wife he would look back on with regret. The first occurred when he was not yet five. Robert had convinced his father to buy him some baby ducks. He delighted in herding them around the yard with a stick. One day, he accidentally struck one of them too hard in the head, killing the duckling. For days he was inconsolable. He made a vow never to mistreat another animal. Even at this tender age, Robert showed an uncanny ability to learn from his mistakes.

The other unhappy incident occurred when the young Spencer was around six and it, too, had a significant impact on the rest of his life. His eight-year-old brother had contracted diphtheria. This serious bacterial disease causes high fever and difficulty in breathing, and it is highly contagious. During the 1890s there was little that could be done medically except to wait and hope for recovery. As a precaution, young Robert was moved out of the house to the barn. Out there alone and scared, he prayed, as his parents had taught him, for his brother to recover. Then one night, a tremendous thunderstorm blew in, buffeting the barn with wind and rain, trapping the terrified six-year-old inside. That was the night, he told his wife, that he prayed like never before. That was the day that his grief-stricken father came to him in the middle of the night to tell him his brother was dead.

It would be inaccurate to state categorically that this was when Robert Spencer lost his faith in God. He was an avowed atheist and freethinker throughout most of his adult life. It was, however, definitely the beginning of a rift between what he had been spiritually taught and what he would actually believe. The idea of questioning his beliefs was conceived here and would undergo a kind of metamorphosis as he grew older. At the time, Robert did not openly disagree with his parents, and he continued to attend church. As he told his wife Eleanor, he went to church after that because the minister allowed him to play pool on his billiard table following the service and let him hand out the songbooks to the church members. He would in time grow to abhor all organized religion.

Robert's high school days were just as happy as his younger ones. Older now, his father allowed him more freedom to enjoy his love for the outdoors. Camping trips became longer as he fished and went on snake-hunting expeditions miles away. Usually he sought out poisonous snakes, releasing them when he had finished examining them. One of his favorite haunts was a place called Charter Oaks, where he met and became friends with an old farmer. It was a remote area in the valley and Robert loved it because of its seclusion. He remembered fondly in later years spending many an hour sitting on the farmer's front porch talking. In his later years he once took Eleanor back to show it to her and they were both surprised to find the dilapidated, abandoned house still there with the front porch intact.

The local Williamsport newspaper followed the exploits of young Robert Spencer and he was often featured in it. One article, when Robert was a high school lad, chronicles how he and a friend shot and killed a several-hundred-pound bear in the mountains near their home. A picture of the bear hanging in the woodshed accompanied the article.

PLUCKY BOYS SLAY BIG BEAR IN THE FOREST

Douglas Spencer and John Hess have rare luck.
Hunting on Wolf Run they vanquish bruin.

The boys were far in the woods when they came upon a 202 pound bear which they succeeded in killing after an exciting fight in which the bear attempted to escape, but their trusty rifles soon brought him to earth—arrived home Wednesday with their quarry.

Douglas Spencer, son of District Attorney and Mrs. Spencer of 74 Washington Street, and John Hess of 813 Mulberry Street, are the proudest boys in Williamsport, for they returned Wednesday from a hunting expedition with the carcass of a 202 pound black bear as a trophy of the chase.

The boys went from this city to Cogan Station, and from that point worked their way out to Sullivan's Drift on Wolf Run. They were accompanied from Cogan by Henry Drill.

On Monday while deep in the dense forest that covers the mountains in that vicinity they discovered the bear—a huge black specimen. Hess was the first to draw a bead on the dangerous game, and fired a bullet which penetrated the bruin's neck. The shaggy animal roared in astonishment and pain and then started to run. Douglas and Hess had their trusty rifles, however, and as the bear attempted to scurry away he found himself under a fire too hot to withstand, and was forced to turn.

All the time the boys were keeping up a steady fire, and bullet after bullet was penetrating the hide of the forest denizen. Suddenly the bear turned and ran about fifty feet, then sank down and succumbed.

The three boys then carried the heavy carcass across the ridge for a long distance, and started out in search of aid. This was readily found and the carcass was conveyed to the railroad station and brought home.

The bravery of these boys, who are from 14 to 15 years of age, is much commented on.

The bear was hanging up in the woodshed at the Spencer home on Washington Street yesterday, where it was viewed by hundreds of people.

During several summers while in high school, there was a special treat. Robert had an uncle who lived and prospected for gold in Colorado. Robert was allowed to spend several summers with the old man and his mule. Together they traversed most of the state prospecting for gold. Spencer kept some of it and later had a gold watch made from it which he gave to his second wife, Eleanor.

Robert's obsession with the outdoors disturbed his father, who feared that it was detracting from his schoolwork. The elder Spencer told his son that if he didn't soon start reading and studying more, he was going to miss out on many opportunities. Robert, a strong-minded young man, respectfully protested and his father usually lost the debates. The boy was near the top of his class in spite of it. Plus he had a mind and personality like that of his mother. When he made up his mind about something it was next to impossible to deter him. All who knew him pointed to this trait as a signature characteristic of the maturing Robert.

Intellectual debates were something Robert Spencer relished until the day he died. He would indulge in them wherever he could find a willing ear. Whether it be the local medical association (which he was expelled from eventually), the Ashland Rotary meetings, in his clinic office, or halfway around the world with a total stranger while on one of his famous trips, he enjoyed the sparring of a good verbal confrontation. Compromise symbolized defeat to him. If convinced he was right, Robert Spencer always stayed the course.

Late in Robert's high school years, William Spencer ran for and was elected District Attorney for Lycoming County on the Republican ticket. Robert was a diehard Republican all his life. He cut short his vacation in 1960 to get home in time to vote for Richard Nixon. One of his greatest thrills was being mistaken for Dwight Eisenhower in a drugstore in New York City. The crowd that gathered outside was sure it was "Ike." He had to leave by the back door.

After high school, Spencer enrolled in nearby Pennsylvania State University. The rural Center County school suited him well. The university was predominantly an animal husbandry and agricultural science-oriented school at the beginning of the twentieth century. Its rustic location and emphasis on the sciences was the perfect match for the budding young scholar. Over the next four years he spent much time outdoors in the Nittany Mountains enjoying his love of nature. Many of the mounted insects and small animals that would later adorn his private study were collected while on these excursions. He performed the taxidermy himself.

Much to his delight, William Spencer's son began to turn into a serious scholar. Robert soon began in earnest to move outside his biology major, reading such authors as Thomas Paine, Benjamin Franklin, and Herbert Spencer. As a science major he was naturally introduced to Charles Darwin's *Origin of Species*. The direct conflict of the theory of evolution assaulted the religious beliefs he held so dubiously, further eroding his faith. His search for the "truth" led him to Paine's *Age of Reason*. The flaming liberalism of the French Revolutionist made an impression on Spencer. After reading the work in which Paine vigorously attacked orthodox religions and the Bible, Robert's use for organized religion disappeared altogether.

Acceptance of statements of authority based on pure logic as opposed to faith inevitably lead to the conclusions that Robert Spencer now made. Faith relies on confidence in the belief that

God is responsible for explaining things which we don't fully comprehend—things that cannot be proven any other way. Those who subscribe to logic and logic alone dismiss faith as useless in answering such questions. They accept only statements of authority based on scientifically provable methods. Facts drawn from science lead to conclusions in their philosophy; faith never enters into the equation. He would never again practice organized religion. He would ultimately accept the existence of a supreme force in the universe but never a god. Alas, his Methodist upbringing had finally failed the acid test.

Now he began to seek out every one of the freethinking authors he could find and immersed himself in their works. The volumes produced by the prolific Benjamin Franklin caught Robert's eye. The homey truths and sound logical advice in Franklin's aphorisms and proverbs delighted him. Later his home and clinic would have the walls adorned with these witty sayings. One done in Dr. Spencer's own hand read: "The most important thing in the universe is energy." One from Thomas Paine read: "The world is my country and to do good my religion." Another from Ben Franklin read: "Where there is marriage without love there will be love without marriage." Some others he had on the wall included: "To live is to suffer," "Oh God, give the world common sense. Beginning with me," "Don't follow me, I'm lost," and "Halitosis is better than no breath at all." He noted that Franklin was one of this country's first natural scientists by virtue of his discovery of the natural origin of electricity in addition to being a freethinker like himself.

Perhaps the single most influential writer that Robert Spencer read during this time in his life was that of the English philosopher and his namesake Herbert Spencer. The parallels between the two are nothing short of remarkable. Herbert Spencer's father was of the Wesleyan Methodist religion—a religion Herbert abandoned. As a youngster, Herbert was headstrong and his father found him extremely difficult to reason with. Herbert grew up in a devout

Dr. Spencer as a medical student at the University of Pennsylvania in 1913.
(Courtesy Atty. Harry Strouse)

Christian home, but one in which he was allowed to show great curiosity in the natural world. He later became an agnostic.

Herbert Spencer was the first to coin the phrase "the survival of the fittest" to which Robert Spencer wholly subscribed. "Survival of the fittest" refers to the contention that the natural order of all species on the earth is governed by the domination of the stronger members over the weaker members of any given species. The stronger ones are able to withstand disease, famine, attacks from others, and so forth, in order to pass on their unique genes so that the species lives on. It is nature's way of avoiding extinction.

Dr. Spencer as a young officer in the U.S. Army. (Courtesy Atty. Harry Strouse)

Apparently, this concept appealed to Spencer's personal philosophy. Herbert's philosophy had two dominant themes that appealed very much to Robert. The first was the individualistic doctrine of utilitarianism which argued that liberty and happiness are the only goals of humankind. The second was evolution. He postulated that all life unfolds from simple single cells, progressing on to a complex fully grown, highly intricate organism. Herbert Spencer's biggest regret was that he did not reach the concept of natural selection before Charles Darwin.

During the summer of one of his upper-class years, Robert spent time with a doctor who was a friend of the family. He sat with the doctor in his office, asking questions and reading his huge medical books. Spencer went with him on house calls and the doctor explained to Spencer the reasons for his diagnosis of each patient. Robert was moved by the human suffering he encountered and the kindly doctor's efforts to ease it. He went back to Pennsylvania State that fall with a firm goal. He would become a doctor.

Robert told his parents of his choice and they were both pleased. Their son would help alleviate pain and save the lives of many people. They had no way of knowing that he would probably be known for terminating more lives than he would save.

In the spring of 1911, Robert Douglas Spencer graduated with honors from Pennsylvania State University with a degree in biology. He applied to several medical schools and was accepted by all of them. He chose the University of Pennsylvania Medical School in Philadelphia, spending the next four years studying hard to realize his dream of a medical career. Robert came home to Williamsport whenever he could to see his parents and keep them updated with his steady progress.

In the course of his studies at the University of Pennsylvania, Robert naturally witnessed a number of people die. Still wrestling with his religious teachings he tried an experiment. Each time he knew someone was about to die, he found some inoffensive way to weigh them. Then, after they died, he would weigh them again, trying to establish if they were lighter after death due to the passing on of their spirit. Sometimes they would be lighter; other times heavier. When a body decomposes gas builds up. If it is expelled the weight decreases and if it remains trapped the weight increases. The measurements are minute. The results were inconclusive and both situations could be explained through science. He arrived at what was for him the inescapable conclusion that human beings had no spirit. There was no God. There was no afterlife. There was only the here and now.

While at medical school, Spencer did something that shook his family to the core. He began to date a young lady. She wasn't just any young lady, she was Jule Butler. Jule's mother and Robert's mother were sisters, which made Robert and Jule first cousins. The families protested but Robert, as usual, was undeterred. Jule was quite taken with him and was accustomed to being somewhat indulged by her parents. Her father was the owner of several lucrative coal mines and was quite wealthy. By the time Spencer graduated from medical school in 1915 they were married.

Robert Spencer wrote to his father around this time regarding where he might intern. The letters were dated March 7, 8, and 9 of 1916. In these letters he uses his father as a sounding board to explore the possible pros and cons of the various hospitals that had offered him an internship. One, he wrote, had less than one hundred beds but offered excellent lab facilities. Another was huge and had nationally renowned doctors on the staff but wouldn't offer him exposure to all of the specialties to which he sought to be acquainted.

Among the facilities he was considering was a hospital at West Chester, Pennsylvania (not far from Philadelphia); one in New York City; one in Patterson, New Jersey; Harper Hospital in Detroit, Michigan; one in Cleveland, Ohio; the Henry Ford Hospital in Detroit; and Blockley (otherwise known as Philadelphia General).

Jule influenced Robert to intern at Philadelphia General. She wanted to stay in the city and enjoy the benefits of society to which her father's money had made her accustomed. After Philadelphia General came some further study at the Rockefeller Institute and a stint in the Army Medical Corps from 1917 to 1918. Dr. Spencer frequently had occasion to go into Washington, D.C., as part of his duties in the medical corps. During these trips he frequented the Smithsonian Institution and the National Geographic Society, and eventually Robert became affiliated with each of them. Dr. Spencer remained a lifelong member of both the Smithsonian and the National Geographic Society.

The years Dr. Spencer spent in the Army were the first years of a wave of flu epidemics that struck both the United States and the rest of the world. The flu epidemic (often referred to as influenza) of 1918–19 killed 500,000 people in the United States alone and 20 million worldwide. Dr. Spencer protested vehemently to the Surgeon General's office that patients stricken with the disease must be given their own clothing, washbasins, towels, and other personal items. He was convinced that the sharing of these common items was contributing to the spread of the disease which was killing people by the thousands. He was later proved to be correct in his diagnosis.

During this same time of epidemic, Robert Spencer received the most devastating blow yet in his life. Word came that his father was gravely ill. Upon arriving home in Williamsport, he found his father sick with the flu. He told his father that daily he was seeing people "dropping like flies" and that it was imperative he stay in bed and take care of himself. His father took the advice lightly and continued to keep his busy schedule as a prosecutor. A short time later he was dead at the age of fifty-nine. A few years earlier he had lost a kidney and this may have contributed to his inability to fight off the disease. Spencer remained devoted to his mother who lived to be eighty-eight. Every Tuesday, until his mother's death, Dr. Spencer would drive to Williamsport to take her out to dinner. Nothing—not rain, sleet, or snow—could prevent his Tuesday ritual. Upon returning from his dinner engagement the doctor would go to his office and see patients until the wee hours, as usual. The influx of patients into the late-night hours were usually the regular ones. The abortion patients were handled first thing in the morning.

Chapter 3

THE LEGACY BEGINS

Even the sadness which I had over my wretched situation was resolved by the profound experience which ended it.

—thankful patient

By 1918, Dr. Robert Spencer left the Army and moved back to Williamsport. He and Jule bought a small house and Dr. Spencer hung up his shingle for the first time. He would always remember his first patient. Ironically, she was a young woman, pregnant, and afflicted with syphilis and gonorrhea. The doctor treated her as best he could by the medical standards of the day, but he knew things did not bode well for the unborn child, who faced a plethora of birth defects. She did not ask for an abortion. The woman had no money so Dr. Spencer treated his first patient for free.

In a short period of time the word spread about the competent and kind doctor. His office was soon overflowing with patients. Some would pay; others couldn't, even though he charged only two dollars for an office visit. After several months, Jule found herself in a situation that both exasperated and embarrassed her. They had no money to pay their bills. She knew Robert was attracting many patients but the lack of money just didn't make sense. When she questioned him he explained that so many of his patients could not pay and he didn't have the heart to force them. To make ends meet, Jule borrowed money from her family, but she made Robert promise to collect his fee from all future patients.

Miners Hospital, Ashland, Pa.

Miners Hospital where Dr. Spencer served as chief pathologist. (Author's collection)

Dr. Spencer tried to keep his promise but his heart just wasn't in it. By the end of the first year of his practice, the pattern kept repeating itself. He treated many patients but had little to show for it. Jule was mortified that there were bill collectors at their door. They argued. She was determined to leave Williamsport, so in 1919 they moved to the city of Hazleton, southeast of Williamsport.

It was a different town but with the same results. The doctor was not a businessman. He was a doctor, he told his wife, and could not see why she made such a fuss if he was helping so many people. Jule could not agree. She pressured him to make sure that everyone paid their bills.

It was in 1919, in the town of Hazleton, that Dr. Spencer performed his first abortion. Strangely, it was at Jule's behest. (She told him she didn't care if he didn't charge this patient.) The young lady was the daughter of a prominent Williamsport family and a friend of Jule's. The young lady had been indiscreet with a young man and found herself pregnant. The scandal would have ripped the family apart. Terminating the pregnancy was the only answer.

Two blocks from Spencer's clinic is this memorial—the only one in the country devoted to mothers and motherhood everywhere. (Author's collection)

Robert was sympathetic to the woman's situation. He could see no sense in forcing her to bring an unwanted child into the world. He probably was also smart enough to realize that with this favor he could score some serious points with Jule. Quietly and quickly the fetus was aborted.

At the end of 1919 the Spencers found themselves broke and in debt once again. Words could not describe Jule's state of mind. This was not the way to begin a marriage and they both knew it. Again Jule turned to her family. Her father's money would once again bail them out of debt while his political connections offered a solution for the future. In 1920 Dr. Robert Spencer was appointed chief pathologist for the Ashland State Miners Hospital in Ashland, Pennsylvania. Here, Jule told her husband, he would have a steady income and the prestige of a hospital staff position. Reluctantly, Dr. Spencer agreed.

From 1920 until his death in 1969, Dr. Robert Spencer's life would be lived out in Schuylkill County. The county's land was pur-

Downtown Ashland circa 1925 when Spencer began his medical practice.
(Courtesy Historical Society, Ashland)

chased from the Delaware Indians in 1749. In 1811 the county was legally formed and named after the headwaters of the Schuylkill River which flowed through it on its way to Philadelphia and the Atlantic Ocean. Following the county's formation, the single most important factor in its growth was the discovery of coal. Timberman Necho Allen is given credit for this discovery. In 1790 he is said to have been on an expedition for good timberland. One night he camped under a ledge at Broad Mountain and built his fire. By early morning he was awakened by a great sensation of heat and light. He had accidentally ignited an exposed section of coal.[1]

Over time the economic value of coal was realized both as a source of domestic heat and for use in the steel industry. Production expanded from a few wagon loads to a point where one million tons could be gouged from the earth in a single week. One vein alone discovered in Schuylkill County was over fifty feet thick of pure anthracite coal. It was dubbed the "Mammoth Vein" and made millionaires out of those who could exploit it.

The first thing you see when entering Ashland from Route 61 is its shrine to mothers. The shrine was built from public donations after local citizens realized how many mothers had lost sons, husbands, and brothers in the various wars.

In 1920 Ashland was a small mining town of about six or seven thousand proud people. Most of the residents were mixtures of German, Irish, Italian, and Ukrainian stock who worked in nearby mines. Protestant and Catholic churches abounded along with many barrooms. The Republican Party dominated the scene and people were decidedly conservative on social issues. The main street, called Center Street, ran north and south through the middle of town for about a mile. Most of the town's commercial enterprises were on Center Street. Dr. Spencer would eventually set up shop at 531 Center Street. The avowed abortionist and self-proclaimed freethinker and Ashland were indeed strange bedfellows.

But for the years 1920 to 1925, Dr. Spencer was the chief resident pathologist at the Ashland State Miners Hospital. It would be a few years until he opened his clinic. The hospital was started and run by the state to attend to the injuries and diseases of the men who worked the mines. There was seldom an empty room at the hospital due to the many accidents at the poorly run coal mines. In this environment of need Dr. Spencer immediately made his presence known. He worked long days and into the night helping the doctors diagnose their patients and chart a course of treatment. He ran the hospital's lab like he lived his life, with great energy, insight, and decisiveness.

Initially the other doctors did not like Dr. Spencer very much. He failed to conduct himself with sufficient tact when differing with his associates. Spencer often disagreed with the other doctors' opinions and told them so. They were not accustomed to being treated so matter of factly. They soon learned, however, that he was seldom wrong when issuing a diagnosis or developing a plan of treatment. He quickly earned their respect and confidence if not their love and was credited with saving many lives while at the hospital. It was while employed at the hospital that Dr. Spencer met and befriended Steve Sukunda.

NOTE

1. *History of Schuykill County* (New York: W. W. Munsell, 1881).

Chapter 4

THE EDUCATION OF STEVE

I shall always be deeply obligated to you for your kindness to me and your understanding. Life assumes again a promise for me rather than a threat.

—grateful patient

S teve Sukunda was born in Yugoslavia in 1892, and was the first of four children. His father farmed a small seven-acre piece of land in the central district of that country. Steve quit school in the fifth grade to help his father work the farm. One day he told his father he wanted to go to America to seek his fortune. The father sold off three acres to get the money for passage on a freighter for his oldest son.

At the age of seventeen, Steve Sukunda arrived in New York City in 1909 with a few dollars in his pocket and hope for the future. He was no stranger to hard work but because he possessed no special skills Sukunda began to wander around looking for employment as a laborer. Standing only five feet, one inch and weighing only one hundred and fifty-five pounds he went from job site to job site trying to convince the foreman in garbled English that he would do the work of two men if given the chance. Before the end of that first day in New York he got his chance. He landed a job on a construction crew for the railroad thanks to a fellow Yugoslavian who did some impromptu interpreting for the foreman. Young Steve couldn't thank him enough.

Like most construction gangs at the turn of the century, this one was composed mainly of immigrants. A majority of them had a considerably better command of the English language than he. Steve was embarrassed at first to open his mouth. Soon, however, through his association with the crew, he not only improved his English but learned some Polish and Italian as well.

Steve was assigned a job as a railwalker. He would get up each morning at four-thirty in order to be on the job at five. His task was to walk a seven-mile stretch of track, heavily loaded down with a bag of tools and a supply of iron spikes. He was to inspect every foot of the seven-mile stretch. If new spikes were needed to secure the rail to the tie he would install them. If a new tie was needed, he was directed to identify the location and notify the road crew to fix it when he returned. For all his efforts, Steve received the meager sum of eighteen dollars a month—twelve of which went for room and board at the railroad camp.

There wasn't much Steve wanted to spend the six remaining dollars each month on so he saved them. There was never a shortage of beer and card games each night. But they held no interest for him. He never drank, smoked, or gambled and he wasn't about to start now. Steve's only vice seemed to have been a "sweet tooth." On the rare occasions when he was in town, Steve could not resist passing a local bakery for a cookie or some pastry.

The road crew winged its way west into Pennsylvania and then south into Maryland and Virginia over the next several years, taking Steve along with it. After six years of this rail work he crossed the Ohio border back into Pennsylvania and toward Pittsburgh. It was here in Pittsburgh that Steve contracted typhoid fever. For weeks he remained in serious condition, too sick to even move. Eventually the fever broke and he began to recover. When he started to feel better, Steve occupied himself by helping the doctors and nurses take care of other patients.

Steve had a natural empathy for the suffering of others and found that he truly enjoyed this role. It gave him a sense of belonging that he could only remember when he thought of his

Steve Sukunda and Eleanor Becker Spencer. (Courtesy Atty. Harry Strouse)

family back home in Yugoslavia. He took orders well and proved to be a great help to the hospital staff. As he eventually prepared to leave the hospital, one of the doctors approached him with an offer. The doctor asked him where he planned to go and what was he going to do? Steve answered that he didn't know. He guessed he'd just start looking for work again. The doctor replied that since he knew the hospital routine and everyone was so sad to see him leave, would he stay on at the hospital as an orderly?

Steve was overwhelmed by the offer, accepting it on the spot. The work was not nearly as hard as the railroad, plus it gave him a chance to use his mind. He stayed on for several years. During this time he displayed the same vigor he had on his railroad job. He received raises and earned the respect of his coworkers. Within months he had moved from orderly to also working in the lab.

As satisfying as all this was it still wasn't enough for Steve. He wanted more. The hospital was a big place. There were many other workers with more seniority than him and who possessed a much better knowledge of the language. He couldn't help but think that a better future lay somewhere else. He kept his eyes open for an opportunity.

Then one day, almost as if fate owed him a debt, Steve Sukunda saw his chance. Posted on the bulletin board was the notice of a vacancy for a lab assistant at the Ashland State Miners Hospital. He sent in an application along with letters of recommendation which he easily obtained from members of the hospital staff. Within minutes after speaking to him, Dr. Spencer offered Steve the job. Little did Dr. Spencer or Steve Sukunda know in 1920 that they would be a team for the next half a century.

Dr. Spencer marveled at how quickly Steve learned his trade. Proof that Spencer taught him well is evident in this interesting anecdote. While working at the hospital, Steve took up residence in a boardinghouse in Ashland. At this house he became friends with another boarder who was a coal miner. The man had a nasty guttural cough which started Steve thinking. One day Steve asked the man why he didn't see a doctor for the cough. The man as much as told Steve to mind his own business. Steve resorted to a little chicanery. He told the man that if he spit in a jar a few times he would take it to the hospital and make a serum from it that would clear him up.

Taking the jar to the hospital lab, Steve prepared a slide the way Dr. Spencer had taught him. He was looking through the microscope when Dr. Spencer came in. When he asked Steve what he was working on the assistant told him and showed him the slide. They both now knew what Steve had suspected. The man at the boardinghouse had tuberculosis. The next day Dr. Spencer examined the man, confirmed his diagnosis, and informed the board of health. The man was removed from the boardinghouse and sent to a sanitarium in the nearby town of Hamburg, Pennsylvania. Steve was saddened to learn a few months later that the man had died. The disease had been caught too late to save him.

This situation underscored to Steve the importance of timely and thorough work by a lab technician. It also impressed the doctor. Dr. Spencer made Steve an offer he couldn't refuse. Spencer called the University of Pennsylvania and arranged for Steve to enter school there to study to become a lab technician. He helped Steve finance the two-year program and put him on the train from Pottsville to Philadelphia on December 24, 1925. There Steve would study under the tutelage of the famous Dr. Kolmer. In fact, Steve performed so well in the program that when he finished, Dr. Kolmer asked him to stay on at the University of Pennsylvania as his assistant. Steve was very grateful for the offer but said, "Doctor Spencer is waiting for me back in Ashland. I must go back."

Chapter 5

SPENCER CLINIC
OPENS FOR BUSINESS

*It is beautiful to find a human being who lifts an experience to one
of dignity and fineness. I shall never forget your humanity.*
—an indebted patient

I t was around the time Steve Sukunda left for Philadelphia
that something occurred that served as a catalyst to
encourage Dr. Spencer to open his own practice again. Hospital
politics caused the removal of the hospital's administrator and his
replacement was charged with the unpleasant duty of cutting costs
and salaries.

There was no denying that the hospital had been operating in the
red. Local politicians saw to it that many of the hospital's services
were rendered free to the local miners and their families. It was the
least they could do and it didn't hurt their chances at the polls come
election time. This was how things were done in the coal regions.

Dr. Spencer was the first one called in to see the new administrator. His abortion stance was already known and his appointment as head of pathology had been rumored to be politically
motivated. The administrator told him that his salary would be cut
by five hundred dollars. Dismayed but never at a loss to make fast
decisions, Spencer replied that if the salary cut occurred, he would
resign. He was told he should do whatever he felt necessary. The
notice of salary reduction came through and was followed the next
day by his resignation.

Dr. Spencer enjoyed his job at the hospital. The problem was he still dreamed of establishing his own practice again. The hospital job was challenging but it was too cut and dried. He couldn't interact with a microscope or slides. He longed to be intimately involved with his patients. He seized upon this chance to convince Jule that he should resume private practice. The salary cut was not only a slap in the face but would hamper them financially as well. She agreed. In 1925 Dr. Robert Spencer was back in private practice.

Dr. Spencer stood no more than three inches over five feet. He was built somewhat like a teddy bear and had a face to match. He wore glasses and a beret on his head each day as he walked the several blocks from his home to his clinic. Everyone knew and greeted the smiling, amiable doctor on his way to work. It was a scene that could have been depicted on the cover of the popular *Saturday Evening Post* by Norman Rockwell.

Dr. Spencer immediately won the hearts of the coal miners and their families with his devotion to their plight. Working in the mines was grueling and hazardous and safety regulations were almost nonexistent. They only slowed up production and cut into profits. When the whistle blew in town, everyone knew disaster had struck at the mine again. There were explosions, cave-ins, gas buildups, floods, and machinery-related deaths and injuries just to name a few. As the women rushed to the scene, the only question to be answered was how many of them would become widows that day.

From 1870 to 1949 there were 30,068 deaths in the mining industry in Schuylkill County alone.[1] In the 450 square miles of the county that's an average of 375 deaths per square mile! In 1925, the year Spencer began work in Ashland, there were 496 deaths. It wasn't until 1982 that Schuylkill County recorded its first year ever with 0 deaths. The "bootleggers" faired even worse than those who worked in the company mines. Bootleggers were independent miners who stole onto company land and sunk their shafts to get at the black gold. Their hurry-up makeshift mines made them espe-

*The Spencer Clinic today, still standing although vacant,
looks much as it did in the 1950s. (Author's collection)*

cially susceptible to a high death rate. It's easy to comprehend how
the United Mine Workers Union Local in Schuylkill County was one
of the union's most powerful strongholds in the country.

Unlike the other doctors in the area who waited at the hospital
when a mine accident occurred, Dr. Spencer grabbed his bag and

rushed to the scene. His presence on site as well as his skill and decisiveness saved many a miner's life. He did more than his share of suturing, setting bones, amputating, and removing crushed kidneys and spleens. Understandably, the miners were devoted to him. He championed many a miner's claim for compensation when they could no longer work, further endearing himself to them.

Dr. Spencer became an expert on the miners' lung disease *anthrasilicosis*, or "black lung" as it was known as among the miners. In those times, miners did not wear masks and were forced to go back into the mine after setting off a charge of dynamite to loosen the coal and rock around it. The light black dust settled in their lungs and accumulated over time. The miners suffered a horrible fate in retirement—gasping for breath, coughing up the black scum, and sleeping upright in a chair. Dr. Spencer became a pioneer in the treatment of this disease for which there was no cure. The success of Dr. Spencer's medical practice was assured. In Ashland and Schuylkill County he had already made a name for himself.

Shortly after Dr. Spencer opened his clinic in Ashland, Steve Sukunda returned to him just as he promised he would. He still spoke in broken English but now he knew his way around a laboratory as well as anyone. Sukunda and Spencer teamed up for the next forty-four years, working seven-day weeks, twelve to fourteen hours a day, interrupted only by trips the doctor spontaneously took when the wanderlust struck him or when the authorities were paying close attention. The clinic at 531 Center Street was open for business.

The stone-facade building was as mundane and ordinary-looking from the outside as any other structure on the street. On the left side it was attached to another similar-looking building. To the right was an empty lot. Inside there was a whole different scene. The front door opened to a large rectangular waiting room which the doctor furnished with the usual chairs and tables. Barely visible to those in the waiting room was a long hall running the length of the building with various rooms on each side.

Dr. Spencer with one of his new-fangled machines in August 1955.
(Courtesy Atty. Harry Strouse)

The first cubicle on the left was an examination room. Next to it was a room with many shelves containing a variety of drugs and chemical compounds. The third held a number of sophisticated-looking machines, some of which Spencer himself designed and had built. The end of the hall emptied into a square-shaped room that served as Steve's laboratory. It was well equipped. An X-ray area and small darkroom stood to the side since Steve took all the pictures and developed them himself right on the premises. Coming back down the hall on the opposite side was a bathroom, a combination examination/washroom, an enclosure in which both Steve and the doctor mixed the salves and prescriptions, and the doctor's consultation room containing his desk and his files.*

The combination examination/washroom was one of Dr. Spencer's inventions. It was used primarily with pregnant women and patients with venereal diseases. Its most unique feature was

---

*After Spencer's death, on advice of counsel, his wife burned these files.

The Roxy Theater in Ashland directly across the street from the Spencer Clinic.
Movie stars whose pictures ran in this theater came to Dr. Spencer for abortions
(not the two on the marquee, however). (Courtesy Historical Society, Ashland)

the sink custom made to his specifications. The construction of it was such that the patient could sit directly on it with both legs spread apart, resting in heel indentations put there for that purpose. It enabled the patient to sit while washing the vital area clean. The patient was then in perfect position for the doctor's examination. When dealing with large numbers, efficiency was important.

An elaborately equipped operating room, complete with its own power source, was situated just on the other side of the right wall of the waiting room. A heavy dark-green curtain separated the operating room from several smaller recovery rooms. The shaded windows of these rooms looked out onto the main street of town. Thousands of women would lay here recovering from their abortions, listening to the shuffling footsteps and muffled voices of the townspeople only feet away. The second floor housed a room with a leather couch on which Spencer would rest when working late or when spending the night to see a patient through a crisis. The third floor contained an apartment which was rented out to a quiet, elderly gentleman.

Externally the building attracted no attention. All around this rather ordinary structure life passed it by with benign neglect. Everyone knew what went on inside but chose to ignore it. Directly across the street stood a snack shop that was a hangout for the town's teens. Several doors down the street from it was the town's lone movie theater called the Roxy. Next to the snack shop was an antique store that derived most of its revenue from the out-of-town visitors to the Spencer Clinic. In fact, most of the business enjoyed by the drugstore, the restaurant, and the hotel were directly attributable to Dr. Spencer's clinic. The proprietors of these establishments were very critical of Spencer's abortion practice, still, none of them ever turned away a customer. All of them became reasonably wealthy while the doctor struggled financially to keep his clinic doors open.

The rear entrance to the building was even more unobtrusive than the front. There was simply a plain-looking door between two garage doors identified only by a small piece of paper taped to the curtained window announcing "Spencer Clinic" typed on it. Across the alley was an old abandoned warehouse. Down the alley, only three garages away and in plain view, was the Ashland Borough Hall and Police Station. By late afternoon on a summer day, the shadow cast by the police station virtually cloaked the entrance to the clinic in shade. For decades these two institutions, one sworn under oath to uphold the law, the other driven by conviction to violate it, coexisted within yards of each other.

NOTE

1. Research done by Edward Conrad for a wall plaque in Zion Lutheran Church, Minersville, Pennsylvania.

Chapter 6

A MAN
AHEAD OF HIS TIME

I want you to know that it isn't just that you were instrumental in giving me another chance to work out a better way of life, but that the manner in which you did it strengthened my belief that there can be goodness and human love in this world of violence.

—appreciative patient

Not long after his return to Ashland, Steve and the doctor settled into a smooth working relationship at the clinic. Dr. Spencer expertly saw to the patients while Steve just as deftly performed all the tasks required of him in the laboratory. They both were usually so engrossed in their work that sometimes they hardly spoke to each other all day, giving rise to a rumor that they did not get along. When I asked Steve about this he laughed so hard I thought he might hurt himself.

Steve described the doctor's activities in the clinic like those of a bumblebee, quickly moving from one patient to another all day long and into the night, as if the rest of the world didn't exist. Steve once said to me each day was like an hour. Each week like a day. The days were long ones. The doctor would be in the clinic by seven each morning; earlier if there were a number of serious operations. Steve usually arrived before him to begin preparing for the day ahead. Lunch was grabbed on the job and quitting time was rarely before midnight or later.

Dr. Spencer's long hours were the result of people's confidence in his ability to help them no matter what their problem was. Their expectations of his availability to them was a direct result of his dedication to helping anyone who came through his door.

I was told by numerous people that if you walked into the clinic at 11 P.M. you could fully expect to find yourself in a packed waiting room. It was not unusual for Dr. Spencer to spend an hour with a single patient, quietly listening to his or her troubles and fears, then dispensing both psychological and medical advice. He would even gladly discuss the nonexistence of God if you wanted. Afterward he might administer two or three packages of pills and extort the outrageous fee of two dollars for his services. If the patients claimed they had no money the doctor believed them and gave his services for free. In fact, they might well find a bag of groceries on the doorstep the next morning.

Over time, Steve expanded his expertise and became somewhat of a legend in his own right. In addition to doing the usual blood and urine tests, he took it upon himself to take and develop X rays, read them, give injections, prepare slides for the doctor, assist the doctor in operations, as well as mixing prescriptions and ointments. He became an expert in the treatment of skin disorders. He may not have been a dermatologist, but many a person told me that after finding no relief from various skin specialists, Steve succeeded in solving their problem. He would examine them and then mix up his own salve. By the time they returned to him they were on their way to being cured.

Down through the decades Dr. Spencer was sent patients by numerous other doctors as well as by word of mouth. The referrals came from as far away as California to the west and England to the east. Most doctors, aware of his controversial reputation, avoided any personal contact with him. They chose, instead, to verbally direct the women they could not help his way. This never affected the dedicated doctor. He eagerly treated all who came through his clinic door—whether the front or the back.

As a diagnostician, Dr. Spencer stood head and shoulders above his peers. Many of his patients were referrals from doctors in other towns and cities. As his reputation as a doctor spread, the number of referrals steadily increased. In spite of his confidence, Dr. Spencer did not hesitate to refer the rare patient he couldn't diagnose to someone who might be able to help. He never let money or ego interfere with sound judgment.

Fortunately for me, Robert Spencer wrote everything down and saved everything sent to him. I was therefore able to read through the many letters sent to him from doctors and hospitals to which he referred patients. Most of them contain generous compliments about his accurate diagnosis of often difficult cases. Some of his colleagues were quite frankly in awe of him.

Places he referred patients to included the Cornell University Medical School, the University of Pennsylvania Hospital, Jefferson Medical School in Philadelphia, Walter Reed Medical Center in Washington, Massachusetts General Hospital, the Geisinger Medical Center near Ashland, and a large number of doctors in New York City and Philadelphia who were specialists. Invariably they confirmed his diagnoses.

Over the decades, Dr. Spencer and Steve waded through an almost daily dose of medical challenges that perhaps nobody in today's world of specialization experiences. The doctor learned about black lung or "miners' asthma" and his clinic was the place to go for treatment. The miners kept him busy in other ways as well. The occupational hazards they faced ensured a constant supply of patients to the doctor.

In the clinic they performed tonsillectomies, and removed prostates, tumors, and appendixes. The doctor helped the local dentist remove teeth from serious heart patients in the clinic when no one else would help them. Spencer developed an injection that would shrink a person's hernia, rendering it unnecessary to have surgery. Always reading medical journals, Spencer not only stayed current but often contributed research and inventions of his own. He developed a sophisticated camera to take close-ups of lesions, moles, tumors, etc. The clarity and magnification allowed instant diagnosis of malignancy. The machine had an elaborate lighting system with an ingenious cooling system to keep the powerful lights from getting too hot.

Dr. Robert Spencer was a regular contributor to the *Journal of the American Medical Association* and other medical publications as well. In 1921 he published a paper with *JAMA* titled "A Case of Oriental Sore of Italian Origin Encountered in the U.S." This diagnosis was so rare and unparalleled that not a single example of it existed in the entire country. Both Cornell University and the University of Pennsylvania asked the doctor if they might have the physical evidence of the test used to diagnose so they could employ it in their medical schools to show students what it actually looked like. In 1924 he published "Chronic Fibrinous Bronchitis as a Symptom of Mediastinal Compression" in *JAMA*. I have no idea what it means but Dr. Spencer, when he could find the time, could write like this at will.

Six months before sodium pentothal was approved by the Food and Drug Administration, Dr. Spencer was using it in his operations. As early as the 1930s, Spencer was quietly purchasing radium seeds from the Radium Emanation Corps. in New York City and using them to effectively treat breast cancer. He made incisions at the affected areas and implanted the seeds and thereby avoided the need for radical mastectomies.

He and Steve broke down the new vaccines and prescriptions in their lab. Then, toying with their contents, they developed their own improved versions. Often they came up with an entirely new compound that they used successfully. The doctor, as a result of his contact with literally thousands of patients with venereal disease, became an expert in its treatment. The Spencer Clinic was one of the few places in the country where this socially unacceptable disease could be treated competently and confidentially.

When other doctors were operating to remove kidney stones, Robert Spencer developed his own system of treatment. Using a fluoroscope, he snaked up the urinary tract and grasped the stones, removing them without surgery. If they were too large he would crush and remove them. Today such treatment is commonplace. Back then it was revolutionary.

Dr. Spencer was one of the first doctors in the country to use the bronchoscope, which allowed a doctor to view the chest cavity and locate any foreign objects trapped inside. He spotted it while leafing through a medical journal. That day he put his order in. When it arrived he was like a kid with a new toy. He didn't have to wait long to play with it. The day after he and Steve assembled it, an occasion called for its use. A woman, with a large open safety pin between her teeth, was hard at work as a sewer in a nearby garment factory. Deep in concentration, she wasn't prepared for the loud, shrill dinner whistle. When it blew it startled her, causing her to inhale the open pin. She couldn't breathe and soon began turning blue. Wisely the decision was made to carry her to a car and rush her to Dr. Spencer. The doctor must have been excited as he flipped on the switch and placed the machine in front of her. He spied the culprit and went down her windpipe to the entrance of the lung where the pin was lodged. In minutes he extracted it, literally saving the woman's life.

The local newspaper was constantly chronicling Dr. Spencer's exploits with the bronchoscope. In a very short period of time I uncovered the following stories as examples:

- A five-year-old girl from Mahanoy City swallowed an upholstery tack. Spencer, using the scope, retrieved it.
- An eleven-month-old boy from Hegins ingested a button. Spencer couldn't get it out with the scope so he successfully removed it in an operation.
- A Shenandoah boy took in a paper clip. Spencer withdrew it from the boy's lung without incident.
- A Kulpmont man was showing some friends a magic trick with a dime when he swallowed it. Dr. Spencer got it out.
- In Sunbury a young boy did the same with a rivet. Results were the same; successful retrieval.

Dr. Spencer in his prime uncharacteristically sporting a necktie instead of his usual bow tie. (Courtesy Atty. Harry Strouse)

- Another safety-pin incident was handled. In Shamokin a twelve-year-old girl swallowed a jack playing with her ball and jacks. Chalk up two more successful cases for the doctor.

Dr. Spencer went to Philadelphia to study the use of the bronchoscope under Dr. Chevalier Jackson, its prominent developer. Dr. Jackson later received the nationally prestigious BOK award along with a $10,000 grant for his use of the bronchoscope. In his acceptance speech he said that the award and accolade really belong to Dr. Robert Spencer from Ashland.

Cardiology, gynecology, cancer, venereal disease, pulmonary disease, surgery, dermatology, pharmacology, colon-rectal, urinary tract, and on and on. Dr. Robert Spencer did them all and did them well. Because of this and because of the genuine kindness he showed his patients, the people came from miles around. Oh how they came.

Dr. Spencer was a man who had every confidence in his own abilities. Some people would misinterpret this confidence as arrogance and foolhardiness. A case involving the local dentist will serve to illustrate this point. One day Spencer called Dr. Roberts, a dentist with whom he had a casual friendship. He requested that Dr. Roberts come to the clinic in the late afternoon to give him a hand with one of his patients. Asking no questions, Roberts answered that he would be there.

Upon Dr. Roberts's arrival, Dr. Spencer introduced him to a lady in her early seventies. Spencer told him the woman had five teeth that needed to be extracted and asked Dr. Roberts if he could do the job. The dentist examined the lady's mouth and said the surgery could be done. Spencer inquired how long he estimated the operation would take. About twenty minutes was the answer. Dr. Spencer injected the woman with a general anesthetic and Roberts proceeded with the extractions. Spencer assisted while closely monitoring the woman's vital signs. All went as planned.

After the lady left the clinic, Dr. Roberts began to get suspicious and asked Spencer why he was asked to do this at the clinic instead of sending the woman to his dental office. Spencer told him the woman had a bad heart condition and her doctor wanted to put her in the hospital for about a week before even attempting to pull the teeth. At first, Dr. Roberts was angry at Spencer, but within minutes he was laughing along with him. Spencer knew the woman's condition and knew they could complete the task without incident. She had come to Dr. Spencer asking for his help, telling him she could not afford a week-long stay in the hospital for five teeth, and he knew this to be true. Totally committed to helping anyone who came to him, Dr. Spencer simply could not turn her away.

Spencer's unbridled compassion for his patients is clearly demonstrated in a story Steve Sukunda once related to me. One day a very frightened farmer from the west end of the county came to the clinic with some ominous-looking lesions on his face and scalp. It didn't take the doctor long to diagnose a severe case of skin cancer. Almost shamefully, he confessed to the farmer his limited knowledge and ability to treat the disease. The forlorn farmer pleaded for help. Spencer sent the man away but not before telling him to return in about three weeks' time.

Two days later the clinic was closed and Dr. Spencer was gone. Earlier that week he had read in his medical journal about a doctor doing research on the very skin cancer that the farmer had. For the next two weeks, at his own expense, Robert Spencer was in Chicago taking a crash course under the doctor's tutelage. When the farmer returned, Spencer began to treat him and eventually the farmer was cured. It is worthwhile to note that Dr. Spencer never took a penny of payment from the grateful man. Dr. Spencer's devotion to his trade was profound. He was first and foremost a doctor; next a husband; and third a friend to whoever reached out to him. The cadence of this order never deviated throughout his medical career.

Dr. Spencer's sympathy and equal treatment for all who came to him was legendary. In the early decades of his practice integration of blacks had not yet occurred. Ashland itself contained no blacks whatsoever. Spencer constructed a separate facility some two or three blocks from the clinic where African Americans could stay when in town to avail themselves of his services. It solved a serious problem for these discriminated-against souls who would never be given a room in the all-white town.

While Dr. Spencer was busy saving lives he also took the opportunity to save Steve's as well; not once but twice. The first time occurred when Steve was absentmindedly connecting some internal wires to a newly acquired fluoroscope in the clinic. This was a mounted screen that allowed viewing of the internal parts of the body by transmission of X rays through the body. Forgetting to disconnect the machine from its power source, he paid the price. His bloodcurdling screams brought the doctor at a run. The electrical current had Steve frozen to the machine, jolting him around like he was on an amusement ride. The doctor quickly threw the main switch, freeing Steve who was within seconds of lapsing into unconsciousness. It was Steve's first experience with how dangerous electricity could be. He told me he simply could not believe how powerless he was to free himself from the machine even though he knew he would die if he couldn't. Once the doctor was sure Steve was going to be all right, he gave him a severe scolding. Robert Spencer could not tolerate foolish mistakes from anyone around him and always let it be known.

The second accident Steve suffered at the clinic was much more serious and very nearly ended his life. On this occasion Steve was working on the clinic's X-ray machine. The cover over the machine's lens had come loose. Steve told me he knew the machine was plugged in but said he had been trained that it was unnecessary to unplug it when working on the outside. There must have been a short somewhere within the machine because when he went to tighten the screws that had come loose on the cover, he was electrocuted.

This time he did not scream. Only the flickering lights alerted the doctor of trouble. He found Steve glued to the machine; his clothes and hand where it came into contact with the machine lit-

erally on fire. Again the doctor threw the switch, freeing his asso-
ciate. Now Steve lay motionless, not breathing, and without a
heartbeat. Dr. Spencer resuscitated him and rushed him to the hospital. The hair on Steve's head and eyebrows was completely
burned. His glasses were a molten pile of plastic on the floor. His
right hand had been horribly burned also. Spencer feared the right
hand would be lost. So did the doctors at the hospital. Fortunately,
a Dr. Romualdo Schicatano was called in for consultation. Dr.
Spencer and he were friends. After several months of operations,
grafts, and therapy, Steve recovered full use of his hand and
returned to Spencer's side.

Working late into the night made the doctor a likely target for
thieves. Doctor Spencer and Steve never gave it much thought
until the unthinkable happened. One evening, very late, a man
called saying he had a very sick brother and asked the doctor if he
could bring the man in right away. The doctor told the caller to
bring the patient in and he would be glad to have a look at him. By
the time the two men arrived, the clinic was empty except for Steve
and the doctor. While Steve was in another room in the clinic, the
two men proceeded to rob Spencer, giving him a nasty blow on the
head in the process. The doctor bought a handgun following the
incident and kept it at the clinic. As Steve chuckled to me, "What
good does it do? It's too late to buy a gun after we were robbed."

Ironically, the blow to the head was the second in his career. The
first came when Spencer was about five years old and was living in
Williamsport. The boy's love for animals was insatiable. On one
particular day while lavishing too much attention on a passing
horse, Robert was soundly kicked in the head. He was unconscious
for several hours. When he regained consciousness, he didn't speak
for days, giving his parents quite a fright. As an interesting sideline
to this accident, prior to the kick, young Robert spoke fluent
Spanish. It was taught to him by the family's Spanish housekeeper,
and she said he picked it up in a matter of days. Following the kick
in the head, he could no longer remember a word of Spanish.

Chapter 7

BUSINESS IS BOOMING

I don't know whether you are motivated by purely humanitarian reasons or not, but it makes little difference, because the outcome is so extremely appreciated by everybody. I think you do a great good in the world . . . and thank God you are here.

—a beholden patient

During the 1930s, despite a growing, successful practice (medically if not financially), abortion quickly became the driving force in Dr. Spencer's life. Early on he became convinced that it was a woman's right to control her reproductive destiny. He felt his responsibility was to help the living improve the quality of their lives including performing abortion, if that was what they needed. He remembered his very first patient, the pregnant woman riddled with venereal disease. He recalled the very first abortion he performed on the unfortunate teenage daughter of that socially prominent family. And he recalled being moved by a case his father was involved in as district attorney before Robert even became a doctor.

A girl's father reported that his daughter began receiving threatening letters. She was hysterical. Closer investigation by Spencer's father revealed that she was writing the letters to herself. It turned out that she was pregnant and was desperately trying to draw attention away from her condition. When the true story began to surface, she killed herself. Her grief-stricken father lapsed into depression and eventually completely lost his mind. Robert

Spencer couldn't help but think the whole thing could have been averted by a simple medical procedure, even if it was illegal.

Dr. Spencer was also deeply concerned over the increasing world population and all of its ramifications. As a true man of science he eagerly read everything he could lay his hands on about the problem, especially from the World Council on Population Growth. He didn't at all like what he was reading and hearing. We were birthing ourselves right off the face of the earth.

As the doctor understood it, the massive world population explosion had to be looked at from a historical and scientific point of view. Eons ago the world was covered by oceans from which mountains protruded. Gradually, about three billion years ago, life began to emerge, literally from the energy here on Earth in conjunction with the Sun. Some three million years ago man appeared on the planet. He somehow managed to sustain himself with the renewable energy sources derived directly and indirectly from the Sun. The world's population grew slowly but steadily. It took from the first human being to the year 1800 for the earth's population to reach one billion. The second billion came in only a hundred years; barely the blink of an eye in a cosmic sense. The third billion took a mere thirty years, between 1930 and 1960. Amazingly, the fourth billion was projected to take a paltry fifteen years. At this rate the global population will double to eight billion early in the twenty-first century and hit sixteen billion by midway through it.

The population problem was a basic factor in Spencer's decision to dispense abortions. He had watched this country's population grow from sixty-three million the decade he was born to almost two hundred million at the time of his death. To Robert Spencer, the risk involved in performing an abortion must have seemed small compared to the growing problems of pollution, diminishing resources, the soaring costs to keep pace with them, and the social taboos that kept the laws in place. To Spencer each new life added to the inability of human ingenuity to deal with these difficulties.

Robert Spencer once summed up his whole argument to Steve in this simple equation:

"more people equals more poverty."

He told Steve that at times he was ashamed to admit that he was a doctor. In striving for a miracle, he felt the medical establishment had instead created a monster. By overcoming countless fatal diseases and conditions it gave society a low death rate along with unheard-of longevity. The result was wall-to-wall humanity. Spencer failed to understand why the medical establishment—a group of the nation's elite—didn't come out in unanimous support of contraceptives and abortion as an effective means of birth control.

It befuddled him when he tried to understand how such an intelligent nation could resist change when the world was teetering on the brink of disaster. He scoffed when people bragged about how much more advanced and mentally superior we were to other nations of the world. He would quickly recite how Japan halved its annual birth rate in a decade using legalized abortion initiated in 1947. He pointed out how the Soviet Union and some other European nations had long used abortion as a means of birth control.

This letter, among many that he sent out to various organizations, was sent to Pennsylvanians for Freedom of Choice in Family Planning in 1967.

Robert D. Spencer, M.D.
531 Center St.
Ashland, PA.

First let us look as the world sees the problem. The population explosion is here. The League of Nations should be our authority of what to do. All laws that exist are by no means good ones. The time they believed in witches, and had them burned at the stake illustrates one. Any law that makes the fundamental law take a backseat, in my mind, is a bad law especially when it deals with private affairs."Do unto others as you would have them do unto you." In India it is said that 100,000 may starve in one day. Our medical schools get their skeletons from India meeting such a death, as in this manner a skull is obtained with all the teeth. Who is responsible for the population explosion? Scientists, they have been successful in getting the upper hand of diseases that in the past would eliminate millions: black death, typhoid fever, cholera, smallpox, and many others. The scientists dealing with the explosion paid their part. So the most destructive force they fear to use, as it could eliminate life on Earth. These acts have upset the balance of nature regarding man. So we have vast numbers of people. Since the scientist is responsible for this trouble, he should be the one to solve it. No help is needed from the clergy or politicians; they are not trained in the fields and would only make trouble. The population explosion is the question, the answer is using all methods we have to prevent pregnancy. Abortion will be outstanding as one method to rely upon when the others have failed. This will bring up two big questions: Is it murder? Is it moral? An embryo is no more a human being than an acorn is an oak tree. Many facts must take place before it reaches maturity. Zoologists look upon an embryo as a parasite. At this phase of the question we must remember what the biologists told us, for they know their field: "We are headed for death by starvation." In 1912 a former teacher of mine, and a Nobel Prize winner in medicine made this remark, "No human being has a right to bring misery to another human being, still less that of procreating destined to suffer misery," Dr. A. Carrell.

The moral problem I would have the dictionary solve, rather than the clergy, for many religions exist that have different points of view. The dictionary states what the majority believe in is moral. So India, China, Russia, Japan, Australia, the majority of people on Earth. With this evidence, the League of Nations should back this argument. It is for the good of humanity. United States of America and Canada the most backward English-speaking nations solving this problem. Life is cheap; zoologists will tell you all forms of life must produce many offspring if the species is to survive. Look at the human species; the vast numbers of which are destroyed in war. Remember that life is fed by death; even in the remote past warriors ate warriors. Those that believe in creation must realize that murder is the basis for life, for one form of life eats another. We must remember, too, that many human beings will face starvation or some type of a nervous breakdown, as the biologists have demonstrated with various animals. These conditions in a fully developed human, having all his normal senses, can't be compared with abortion, where [in a fetus] these senses are not developed.

As I see it, we are still in battle—the world of reality against the world of myth. One we can see the results, the other requires blind faith, with no evidence to support the faith. When reason is killed what is the use of education? Those who try to explain myth, teach ignorance. They have no facts to support their argument.

So let us do our family planning with a normal educated brain.

He used to say that if an outbreak of malaria occurred in Pennsylvania tomorrow, a massive medical campaign to combat it would instantly begin. Yet, each year only a handful of women with the money can find a way to get an abortion, forcing thousands of others to go the route of the back-alley butcher. Dr. Spencer resolved to do what he could regardless of the criticism and regardless of the law. He would be like the captain of a ship saying "Stay the course and full speed ahead" through five long and difficult decades.

Within this worldview, Dr. Robert Douglas Spencer began in earnest in the 1920s and 1930s to perform abortions. In doing so over half a century he earned the title "The King of the Abortionists" and was recognized as such nationwide. For the first two years after opening the clinic in 1926, Spencer did all the abortions for free. He was determined to maintain this system but reality forced him to reassess. The people began to come to him in such large numbers that he had no choice but to begin charging a fee. If he didn't at least recoup his expenses he would be unable to keep the clinic open. Women began coming from all over the state and beyond. Each woman who came to him received the same kindness and expert care regardless of her socioeconomic status. Each also was made to read a notice on the office wall.

Robert D. Spencer, M.D.
531 Center St.
Ashland, Pa.

You are asking me to help you, we may break a law (this varies, depending on many factors). I feel the statute law broke a much older and better law namely DO UNTO OTHERS AS YOU WOULD HAVE THEM DO UNTO YOU. Abe Lincoln, when he fought for abolishing slavery, remember, had the laws in many states and all religions against him.

Abe Lincoln's religion was to do good. We can have heaven or hell on earth while we are living. We can have peace or war. We will have war if we do not have birth control and war is hell.

I will help you if you will agree to the following:

1. Follow instructions in detail.

2. Return to me in case any unforeseen trouble should develop. You realize nothing can be done that does not invite hazard. You can't eat a meal or take a bath and be certain you will survive. No need to be a pessimist.

I WOULD NOT HELP YOU IF I DID NOT THINK WE WOULD BE SUCCESSFUL. HONESTY AND COOPERATION ARE REQUIRED.

3. DO NOT CONSIDER THIS OPERATION IF YOU ARE NOT CONVINCED IT IS FOR YOUR OWN GOOD. IF YOU THINK IT IS A SIN DO NOT HAVE THE OPERATION.

4. THE FEE FOR THIS WORK IS PAYABLE IN ADVANCE.

5. I DO NOT PERMIT ANYONE IN THE ROOM AT THE TIME OF THE OPERATION.

6. I expect some party with you to act as your nurse and be responsible to bring you back to me if necessary.

7. Do not make any arrangements for parties to contact you by phone at my office.

8. IF I REFUSE TO HELP YOU AFTER EXAMINATION, IT MEANS I THINK YOU ARE NOT A GOOD RISK.

The opening of the clinic coincided with a moral sag that is so typical in a postwar era. A demoralizing effect of the materialism that spread throughout the nation was rearing its ugly head. An obsession with sex erupted as previous taboos were disregarded.

After World War I, skirts rose above the knee for the first time in history. The "half-nude" one-piece bathing suit was born. The decadent jazz age emerged and the "in" crowd wore zoot suits and décolleté flapper dresses while dancing cheek to cheek to the sexy moan of the saxophone.

Each day at the Spencer Clinic the unhappy results of this devil-may-care era of wonderful nonsense came asking for his help. In his log the doctor noted that they came from the country as well as the cities; they were rich and poor; and they were equal in numbers from all faiths. He could discern no pattern, no boundaries. Steve told me the doctor had only one hard-and-fast rule: He would not do an abortion if the fetus was past eight weeks. In some extreme cases, Steve admitted, he might stretch it to ten but no further. Beyond that time frame Spencer considered the procedure too dangerous, citing that his mission was to save and improve the quality of lives, not endanger them.

As a result of the growing numbers at his doors, Dr. Spencer began charging five dollars. He held the line there for years before costs (not profit) caused him to relent and raise it to ten dollars. Over the years, solely due to necessity, it would go to twenty, then fifty dollars. At the time of his death in 1969 the charge was never more than one hundred dollars.

Contrary to popularly held beliefs, abortion is not historically steeped in illegality. In colonial America there were actually no written laws banning abortion. It was rather loosely controlled by common law (unwritten laws handed down over generations). Abortion was permitted as long as it was done before quickening occurred. Quickening referred to that point in time when a woman could feel movement of the fetus (usually around the fifth month). Of course in that era they had no medical way of establishing whether or not the fetus was alive prior to movement. Now, of course, we know different. Even today the longer a woman's pregnancy continues, the less likely she will seek an abortion. Less than 1 percent of abortions occur after the fourth month.

In the 1800s as more families left the farms to move to the industrialized cities, large numbers of children became a burden instead of a boon. One solution was to resort to abortion. By the early 1800s a few laws were on the books in a handful of states solely for the purpose of protecting women from the poisons (herbs, potions, folklore remedies) being used to abort. The mid-nineteenth century saw the formation of the American Medical Association and its attempt to prevent anyone but trained physicians from practicing medicine. Their main targets were the numerous abortionists.

By 1880 there were forty states with laws making performing an abortion at any stage of pregnancy a crime. Stricter laws and improved medical procedure did little to stop the demand for abortions. In 1936 (the apex of the Great Depression when many were destitute) it is reported that 500,000 abortions were performed in the United States. Most were done by the untrained and dirty hands of quacks. It is little wonder that the name of Dr. Spencer became known around the country.

It's not hard to envision the steady growth in Dr. Spencer's abortion business. The fact that for two years he provided his services for free guaranteed that the number of visitors would grow steadily. At first there were the wives of farmers and miners. Along with them came young unmarried girls, married women who were having affairs, and people from fairly prominent families in Schuylkill County.

Soon the word began to spread about the caring doctor from Ashland. People began to arrive from places like Wilkes-Barre, Philadelphia, and Harrisburg. Young women at college who suddenly found themselves pregnant learned about Dr. Spencer and soon the college campus became a major contributor to his business. It wasn't long before most Pennsylvania college students knew the directions to Ashland.

From there the word spread to the contiguous states. Women began coming from New Jersey, New York, Maryland, and

Delaware. Greenwich Village in New York City was to become a major pipeline to the Spencer Clinic over the years. The liberal lifestyle celebrated there often resulted in unwanted pregnancies. These women found Dr. Spencer and passed the word along. For years people in Ashland could tell you how, on a daily basis, the bus would arrive from New York with at least one or two young ladies on it. They would get off the bus and go into Weyman's Restaurant to ask directions to the clinic.

By the 1950s Dr. Spencer had seen women come from virtually every state in the Union plus several foreign countries. He developed a system whereby he assigned his patients a code number that identified data such as their geographical origin, age, marital status, and religion. Although he took down names he was sure most of them were fictitious. He would study this information from time to time to see if he could learn something from it. The only conclusion he could come to was that there were no barriers when it came to getting pregnant.

Over the decades women came from far-off lands as well. Spencer performed abortions on women from England, Switzerland, Thailand, France, and South America. Many of these women, as one would imagine, were wealthy and more than willing to pay many times what Dr. Spencer charged. Despite this temptation the doctor never took payment in excess of his usual fees. The very first day he opened his practice, Robert Spencer decided that he was not in it for profit. He remained faithful to this conviction until the day he died.

The statistics he developed on his abortion patients were telling. Alas, most of his records were burned (both to protect identities as well as to guard against any possible lawsuits) but I was able to gather some basic information. When he first started giving abortions most of the women were married. Most did not want to add any more children to their families (whether the husband was the father or not). In the 1950s he noted that more than half of his patients were single, a definite change in his patient demographics. The average age during this time was also dropping as well.

He was seeing more younger patients than ever before. Dr. Spencer found that women were now bringing their daughters to him for the same reason they themselves came years earlier. Investigation by the doctor revealed that 15 percent of the women he gave an abortion to returned for a second and sometimes a third.

At the start it was through word of mouth that female patients showed up at his clinic. Now he was getting referrals from other doctors, lawyers, high school counselors, college administrators, and even Catholic priests and Protestant ministers. The women were representative of the general population. He served Catholics, Protestants, and Jews alike. There were all races and all socioeconomic classes among his patients. The only common thread he could find was that they did not want to have the child they were carrying.

Statistically speaking, if you take almost one hundred thousand abortion patients over five decades, it stands to reason that there would be some very well known individuals on the list. Indeed, the Spencer Clinic saw many nationally famous people come through its doors. The names of these persons would be instantly recognizable if they were given. I shall not name any of them for it would serve no purpose other than to embarrass families and appeal to the prurient interest of others. The records have been burned and those who personally knew of the true identity of such persons are now dead. However, the following descriptions should give a clue as to the range of notables Dr. Spencer aided.

- Late one night, under the cover of darkness, a five-foot, nine-inch, red-haired actor known for his tough-guy roles brought in a girlfriend who had "missed her mark" and needed the specialized services of Dr. Spencer.
- One of the major trade publications in 1956 had this blonde, green-eyed actress listed as the number-one box-office

attraction. This sometimes moody and insecure actress found her way to Ashland, Pennsylvania.

- A pregnant girlfriend brought this Democratic senator from a Midwestern state to the Spencer Clinic one night. He was rather famous when in office for his severe criticism of bureaucratic waste.
- This tall, thin actor had a shocking head of gray hair and starred in many movies. You may remember him doing commercials for a pharmaceutical company near the end of his career. He knew where Ashland was.

There were many others besides these: state politicians, chiefs of police, district attorneys, doctors, lawyers, judges, school-teachers, and bishops of both the Catholic and Protestant faiths to name just a few.

The malevolent myths surrounding a man such as Dr. Spencer were many. I found all of them to be unfounded. Fear, suspicion, and distaste for the illegality of what he was doing behind those doors on Center Street may have given rise to these rumors. One such myth that sprung up about the doctor in Ashland was that his sewer line was frequently blocked with the discarded fetuses, requiring the local fire company to come and hook up the hoses to the fire hydrant to unblock the line. An attorney who was borough solicitor for twenty-two years during Spencer's practice states cat-egorically that this is pure hogwash.

A second festering rumor was that the doctor violated the women he was performing abortions on. As we all know, this occa-sionally happens in the medical profession—but never with Dr. Spencer. He always treated his patients with the utmost respect, and virtually everyone I talked to about the matter swore that the man was incapable of such an outrage. To be sure, many times his second wife, Eleanor, was present when he was performing these operations. As further proof of his innocence, not one single charge was ever brought against him.

Another story that persisted was that Spencer paid off all of the police in the area allowing him to conduct his activities without interference. According to Steve Sukunda, there were times when the doctor may have become indebted to someone who warned him he was being watched but, Dr. Spencer was not in the habit of paying people off. But generally speaking, the locals kept him informed of police activity out of a sense of obligation (since he had helped so many of them) and respect for the man.

On one occasion the local Knights of Columbus chapter became so incensed at his activities that for weeks they observed the comings and goings of all of his patients. They wrote down numbers of all out-of-state license plates and recorded the names of the out-of-town visitors staying at the local hotel. They turned this information over to the state police and demanded action. The doctor soon received word that the heat was on and temporarily shut down his illegal activity. After weeks of uneventful stakeouts, the state police left empty-handed.

At his peak, Dr. Spencer was doing upwards of ten abortions a day. Whenever a shutdown of his practice was warranted, Spencer, always concerned about his patients, would refer them elsewhere. There was a doctor in New York he sent people to and with whom he regularly corroborated. For those who had the money there was a Dr. Eduardo Elias in Havana, Cuba, where patients were sent. I personally read the letters of correspondence between these two men during such times. In the letters Elias referred to Spencer as "father" and himself as "son." Instructions to patients were very detailed as to what hotel to stay in, which rooms, and how they would be called to the front desk with a taxi waiting out front to take them to their clandestine destination. Dr. Spencer received no remuneration from these referrals, only satisfaction.

Because of the notoriety he was receiving for the abortions, the local Schuylkill County chapter of the AMA censured him. Sukunda could not remember the date but recalled succinctly how they called the doctor before them and berated him. They said his outspoken views and open performing of abortions was an affront to the medical profession. From that point on, he was summarily ostracized from the chapter. Showing no fear, Dr. Spencer stood and boldly defended his position, declaring that in time he would be proven right. His final words were to the effect that they might be able to expel him from the organization but they could not take his license to practice—and continue to practice he would.

It was at this time that he was motivated to write the national chapter of the AMA. What follows is a rough draft of the letter he sent to them which I acquired from Mrs. Eleanor Spencer. It captures both his philosophy and his view of life.

A Pathologist's Point of View about the Abortion Laws

I do not believe that any abortion laws should exist; take the time to read what I write and I will explain why I have taken this attitude. The laws of most civilized countries will stand for protecting life, liberty, and the pursuit of happiness. I am positive that the majority of people believe in love as being a great force for the human race; all religions I believe will back this statement. This word covers a vast field, but most cases, especially in ages from fourteen to fifty years. Love leads direct[ly] to the sexual life, so the pursuit of happiness in man's life and in many of the opposite sex terminates in sexual contact. This driving force of sex is due to chemicals created by the reproductive glands, and as we are mammals we are driven by that force to reach that goal. We have a brain, so do all mammals. We are supposed to have our sex life easily under control. [T]his is impossible unless they have lost the glands that create the drive. People have various grades of brains[;] some are idiots, yet the sex life they know, and they know so well that it made Oliver W. Holmes, Chief Justice of the [U.S.] Supreme Court, make the remark that something should be done about it. He knew of several generations in one family [who made] the country take care of their offspring when laws of sterilization could have prevented [these births]. Let us look at the driving force of sex. [A]t least two popes had sons that became popes. Alexander VI was one of them. We have had two presidents who had sex problems while [in office], and we still have laws that read as though everyone is master of himself. I know from experience priests, ministers, judges, and in fact [persons from] all walks of life make this mistake. We have two driving instincts, hunger and sex: one to keep the individual alive, the other to keep the race alive. The chemical power of sex is stronger than breaks of the brain. This religionists should remember. This is why many high school girls and college girls have sex problems. Their reproductive glands dominate their brains. Criminologists will tell you that [the] greatest crimes that [afflict] priests and ministers are sex crimes. [This] shows [that] people [who are] supposed to have brains and [who are] older than college students still have the same problem. The church will see the younger person crucified because religious morals are broken. This opens up a vast field, as the various religious groups have different morals. Here is where hypocrisy steps in. I believe in what Webster states: morals are what the majority do and believe in. I have been trained as a scientist, spending four years at Pennsylvania State University and four years at the University of Pennsylvania, two years in hospitals, [served] several months in World War I, [and received] training [at] the Rockefeller Institute. A time comes when you must choose a belief. You have two choices. [First,] religion which is a myth or [second,] science which deals with facts. The religionist believes we were created by a god. The evolutionist believes we evolved. [T]he sciences—physics, chemistry, paleontology—all support the evolutionist. The religionist, we will admit, in some cases has spent a few years in training, perhaps more than I had in science. Common sense could tell anybody [that] my choice would be [that of] an evolutionist. [The person] trained in religious matters would follow the course he had chosen. Even if he has no facts to support the viewpoint that religion has taken, he believes in myth, superstition, blind faith, and the Bible, which was written by man and supposed to be inspired by God. I am an evolutionist, hence I am an atheist, it is impossible for me to believe in the God as described in the Bible. A host of people better educated than me had the same belief: Mark Twain, Herbert Spencer, Abraham Lincoln, Luther Burbank, Thomas Edison, Joseph Lewis, Thomas Paine, the Deists, George Washington, Thomas Jefferson, Benjamin Franklin, and many others who signed the

Declaration of Independence. I firmly believe we evolved. Primitive man came to endow all objects, animate or inanimate, with spirits to explain the mysteries that he met. It took understanding, not magic, to allow men to enter into the processes of nature, to reproduce them and control them at will. As man evolved, he refined these visions, myths, and superstitions into religions and philosophies of immense orders. I believe in a supreme power that rules the universe; the only way we have to know about such matters is to study the laws of nature. It appears to me to be some electrical force. The basic structure of all matter is electrical. Has life any meaning? I think the religionists if they are honest would say no. That is why so many churches spend so much time training people for the life to come. Why not use that energy training in the world that we know exists? Why not help humanity instead of the churches? As I see the problem it is that one church would like to dominate the planet. No one denomination has any more pull than any other denomination. Most are very aggressive and they make a great political machine. The politicians always look to the next election, so we find ourselves slowly slipping into the Dark Ages. The church seems to believe that if we keep the people ignorant and poor then they can be led. That is why we have fights about education. Money given to support any religious schools is a violation of our constitution. The Catholic schools are controlled by Rome. One can easily see how our country can be destroyed from within. Our constitution was to protect us from such action. We see our representatives take the oath of office but then they vote to destroy the wisdom of our fathers of this country by giving money to church schools. Church and state should be separated.

I would like to ask the legal profession to answer this question: When you have a bad law, and we have had many, what is to be done? For years we had "The Divine Right of Kings," which was thought to be God's will on earth. This is what happens when religion dominates the law. At the present time we have abortion laws where no two experts can agree. Years ago this country believed in witches, [and] priests, ministers, judges—the so-called brains of the country—believed in [witchcraft]. Was anything done [about it]? No, they continued to burn people at the stake for years. And when the government told us we could not drink, many bartenders violated the law and people were murdered right and left. We had quicker action, though it took years before the law was changed. Looking at this evidence it would seem that if many people violated the law, positive results would happen quicker. As an atheist my consciousness would say this is the wrong method. But history shows it works. The Golden Rule—"Do unto others as you would have them do unto you"—is excellent. Laws that destroy this rule I do not consider good laws. Abortion as practiced in Japan shows clearly that it can solve the problem. When your life's work is in medicine, you are trained to help humanity. Being pregnant is a personal problem, but the happiness of many people may be involved. The party in that condition knows more about it than anyone else. She should decide if she wants any thing done or not. One should not be brought into a troubled world when one is not going to be loved and cared for. A babe is born every second. The top biologists tell us that the population explosion is more important than the atomic bomb. I think we should follow their advice. I think the greatest thing Franklin D. Roosevelt did as president was to listen to Albert Einstein and follow his suggestions, without having Congress know what was taking place. The atomic age was born, and it quickly ended the war with Japan. With proper use of our knowledge of the atom great good can be done; if improperly used, it can terminate our lives. July 12 in the *New York Daily News*, the headlines noted "President's Panel Favors Abortion, Recommended Today Repeal of Laws Making Abortion a Crime." Remember what [the philosopher] Seneca said years ago: religion is regarded by the common as true, by the wise as false, and by the rulers as useful. In conclusion, I believe Thomas Paine's credo is worth repeating. My mind is my own church, independence is my happiness, my country is the world, all mankind are my brothers, and to do good is my religion.

As can be seen from Spencer's letter "A Pathologist's Point of View about the Abortion Laws," the doctor's views were highly controversial. His idea of the natural and unchecked essence of human sexual behavior is in keeping with his position as a man of science. In his opinion, the human instinct to engage in sex is beyond controlling. His disdain for organized religion is very evident. The doctor calls religion a myth and a study in hypocrisy. He has no use for what he terms superstition and blind faith. He feels the abortion law is but one of many bad laws the government has made and calls for its repeal. It was a personal philosophy that his first wife, Jule, never involved herself in and his second wife, Eleanor, embraced after listening to Robert's reasoning.

Chapter 8

THE WOMEN
BEHIND THE MAN

*To find a fellow human of your understanding and broad tolerance
was a joyous thing to me.*

—past patient

Over the course of more than twenty years of marriage to
Jule, the intense effort and considerable amount of time
Dr. Spencer put into his practice took its toll on their relationship.
Apparently Jule no longer enjoyed playing the role of a doctor's wife.
The upper-class existence she had been raised in and which she had
envisioned for herself when she wed Robert never materialized.
Thanks to the doctor's low fees and his failure to collect thousands of
dollars from his poorer patients, he and Jule lived well below her aspi-
rations. Many times they found themselves in dire financial straits, a
situation that plagued Spencer throughout his professional life.

The marriage did result in the birth of two children. William,
their firstborn, was followed by a daughter named Louise. Unfortunately the arrival of these two did nothing to strengthen the
Spencer marriage. The children may in fact have weakened Robert
and Jule's relationship. Both youngsters were born with some kind
of infirmity. William, I am told by Steve Sukunda, was born with
extremely fair skin, bordering on albinism. Steve informed me that
he did not do well in school and had a hard time concentrating and
staying on task. Louise suffered from some form of atrophy of her
one hand and leg.

Mrs. Spencer was said to be quite upset at this and questioned her husband about the part their close kinship might have played in both children's problems. Robert denied the connection citing that both deliveries were difficult ones necessitating the use of instruments (the babies were not delivered by Robert). He reportedly told Jule that the damage they suffered could be due to this and that the fact that the parents were first cousins had nothing to do with it. Jule was not entirely convinced. It is doubtful that Dr. Spencer, deep inside, was either. His knowledge of medicine and heredity surely precluded the idea that what happened was either just an accident or pure chance.

The Spencers quarreled and they drifted apart. Jule began to take extended vacations. Taking her sister along with her, Steve said she would be gone for one to two months at a time. This vexed Robert considerably. He repeatedly told her he wanted a full-time wife, not one now and then. They were unable to work out their differences. The health problems of the children, added to the ever-present financial woes, and two determined people who became committed to pursuits that excluded their mates were bound to result in unresolvable matrimonial discord. Jule left the house for good. On May 16, 1945, their divorce became official.

Dr. Robert Spencer agreed to pay Jule Spencer the sum of $16,000 in their divorce settlement. He also agreed to pay her $300 a month for the rest of her life. In addition, he was to be responsible for the education of the children, and Jule was to receive all the furniture in their house. It was a costly settlement but they were now free to pursue their own interests.

Jule and William moved to LaJolla, California, where she lived until her death. Finding it difficult to get details on the children, I believe William is still alive and living in California. Louise married a doctor and may still be living in suburban Philadelphia. I am told that she was staunchly opposed to her father's abortion trade while William appeared to show little interest in the matter.

It was reported to me that Dr. Spencer told his lawyer to expe-

The second Mrs. Spencer in her prime. (Courtesy Atty. Harry Strouse)

dite the divorce as quickly as possible. No doubt he wanted to be free of Jule for obvious reasons. There was another less known reason as well. Robert had fallen in love with another woman. Her name was Irene Eleanor Becker (Ellie, the doctor called her) and she was soon to become the second Mrs. Spencer. It is safe to assume that the first Mrs. Spencer knew about the second.

I first met and interviewed Eleanor Becker Spencer on the afternoon of July 8, 1970. She was very gracious in welcoming me to her home and most eager to speak about her beloved Douglas. Eleanor was about five foot four, somewhat on the heavy side, with dark and graying hair and teeth that displayed numerous silver fillings.

She told me that she began seeing Douglas after his divorce and that it was at least several years before they married. A number of people who refuse to be identified beg to differ and the records bear them out. In fact, Eleanor and the doctor were seeing each other during the last several years of his estrangement from Jule. Four months after his divorce, on September 29, 1945, Robert married Eleanor Becker. I can only assume that her imaginative recreation of the facts was motivated by a desire to protect her own reputation and that of the man she loved.

Originally Eleanor was seeing Steve Sukunda. They had met at the hospital when she took her ailing father in for treatment. Steve would come to her house (where she lived with her parents) to take her on walks or to sit on the front porch chatting. Whether reluctant to enter into a serious relationship or too tight to take her somewhere and spend money (Steve was notoriously frugal with a buck) the relationship stagnated. Dr. Spencer had met Eleanor through Steve and very much liked what he saw. The doctor asked his assistant if Steve minded if he asked her out. Steve graciously stepped aside and a romance soon blossomed.

Eleanor was seventeen years younger than Robert Spencer. She graduated from Kutztown State College and taught elementary school in the nearby town of Mt. Carmel. She taught for seventeen years but quit shortly after marrying the doctor at age thirty-eight.

Eleanor in the laboratory of the Spencer Clinic where she sometimes helped the doctor.
(Courtesy Atty. Harry Strouse)

Mrs. Spencer told me she was attracted to the doctor because he literally "sparkled with life." He was so full of interest in life and his attitude was so contagious that when she was with him he captured her heart. He was very sure of himself and equally sure that he wanted to spend the rest of his life with her. At thirty-eight Eleanor was confident that the right man had finally come into her life. She never regretted her decision to marry this man who she described as "very kind, very humble, and a man who treated all people alike."

She remembered their honeymoon like it was yesterday. Their first stop was the coast of Maine where he took her whale watching. Then it was on to Montreal, Canada. They had a lovely room with a balcony off the bedroom that looked down on the streets of the city. She fondly recalled going out onto the balcony screaming in jest, "Mother, save me! I'm trapped up here in this room with a madman!" Douglas came out after her and pulled her back into the room where they fell into each other's arms laughing uproariously.

Upon their return to Ashland, Dr. and Mrs. Spencer eased into a marriage that lasted from 1945 until Spencer's death in 1969. She was well aware of his devotion to his practice and to his patients. Over the years she would become not only his lover but his friend and confidante as well. Sometimes he would come home from the office and confide in her. Other times he would be sulky and silent. She knew when to ask about his day and when to remain silent. She was always there for him and apparently they had a healthy, happy marriage.

Eleanor was raised Lutheran. She viewed abortion as something terrible until the doctor reeducated her. She came to the office to listen to the plight of the women who were seeking his help. She decided to assist him one day but got sick to her stomach and had to leave the room. She persisted a second, third, and fourth time, finally overcoming her revulsion. Although she did not work in the clinic on a regular basis, she did go in and help when the need arose, supporting him in his personal quest.

Eleanor Spencer was continuously fascinated by this unusual man she married. She once told someone that he was the only man she knew who could spend two solid hours watching the activities of a trap-door spider, totally mesmerized by its comings and goings. She related a story to me that typified the curious and trained mind of Dr. Spencer.

One spring evening after they were married, Ellie and Douglas were walking hand in hand down an old farm road. Suddenly Ellie jumped aside, frightened by something dead she had almost stepped on. She asked Douglas what it was. "That, my dear, is a deceased member of the rodent family otherwise known as a field mouse," he said as he prodded the carcass with a stick.

"Here's another one," he said, pointing with the stick to a spot several feet away, "that has met with the same fate. Ellie, we have stumbled across the scene of a brutal murder."

"What do you mean 'murder'?" she asked, becoming annoyed at him now.

"Do you see how the skulls of these little animals are mangled?"

"Yes, it's disgusting," she answered.

"Well, that's a dead giveaway. There's only one vicious little animal that eats the brains of its victims and that is the weasel. I'll just bet there's a den somewhere nearby with the homicidal maniac holed up in it," he said to her as he poked around in the brush. Soon he let out a cry of victorious discovery.

"I've found it, Ellie! Come here!"

"Why, he's dead, too," she said, keeping a safe distance from the weasel.

"Yes, I see it all now. He's paid dearly for his crime. Look how discolored and puffed up he is. The mice must have ingested some poison laid out by the farmer to rid himself of these pests. The weasel fell upon them but made the mistake of dining on the toxic brains. As a result he never even completely digested his meal before the mice were avenged."

As Eleanor observed, if a hundred people had walked down that lane, at best, perhaps ten would have seen the dead mice. Only Dr. Spencer would be able to look at the scene and discern the life-and-death struggle that had taken place. It was things like this, she said, that endeared him to her.

Chapter 9

A ZEST FOR LIFE

You have been like a father to me in your understanding, and if it had not been for you I probably wouldn't be alive today.
—former patient

I f there was one thing on this earth that Dr. Spencer enjoyed as much as tending to his patients it was traveling. During his lifetime he managed to see a good bit of the major continents of the world. Sometimes the trips would be impromptu excursions due to the temporary closing of his clinic when he attracted unwanted attention from the authorities. It did not happen often but at times he would be told to shut down the clinic until the "heat was off." Other trips were well planned, avoiding the usual tourist traps in favor of seeking out the unusual. He returned from each trip with specimens from the country's animal life, plants, and minerals. He faithfully kept a scrapbook detailing each journey. To enumerate specifics of them all would comprise a separate book, but I shall try to offer highlights of the most interesting.

In the United States alone, Robert Spencer had been in every state but Hawaii. The New England coast was one of his favorite haunts to watch the great whales. In the Florida Keys he took Eleanor out fishing for marlin and insisted they dine on their catch. He visited down there on at least two occasions and had a necklace made for Eleanor (on the second trip) from the teeth of a shark he

Dr. Spencer the scientist. (Courtesy Atty. Harry Strouse)

caught. Eleanor recalled that he even took her mother along with them on this trip. That meant a lot to her.

The trips did not have to be to some exotic destination for Spencer to derive pleasure. The Jersey Shore could be just as much fun as Peru or Alaska. Once while at the New Jersey shore, the doctor took Eleanor out on a small boat. He was busy dredging the bottom of the ocean floor with a wire basket and examining its contents for evidence of pollution. One haul unexpectedly produced a small squid. Instantly he smiled at Ellie, who knew him well enough to recognize that something unusual would come of this.

Robert fired up the boat's engine and announced they were going ashore. Once on land, he set about trapping a seagull and removed one of its tail feathers. From the squid he extracted the ink contained in its sac and, using the tail-feather quill as a pen, wrote postcards home to his friends and relatives, getting more excited with each one as Ellie stood by in amazement.

Colorado, as you may remember, was near and dear to Spencer's heart. He and Eleanor traveled there several times. The doctor delighted in showing her the many places he'd been with his old prospector uncle and the mule. The West Coast was another trip they made together. They drove from San Diego to the Canadian border and just about everywhere in between. In addition, Spencer went through the South and Midwest, along the Great Lakes, and into the Southwest on hunting, fishing, and specimen-collecting trips.

In Colorado he bagged mule deer. In Montana he hunted rams. Down South, Spencer got a wild boar. From Canada he brought back two moose; one he gave to the Moose Lodge in Mt. Carmel for display. Alaska produced a bear much larger than the one from the Williamsport mountains. A snake-hunting expedition in the Florida Everglades was also successful.

Robert traced the mighty Mississippi on a paddle wheel, boated through the Great Lakes and out the St. Lawrence seaway to the Atlantic, and there were medical conventions in every major city in the country. Eleanor usually went with him to these. She remembered the uncanny ability he had of drawing a crowd around himself within minutes of entering a room. Expounding on his theories and running through a recent medical breakthrough he had made kept the crowd mesmerized.

Perhaps his favorite place in the States was the Grand Canyon. The natural display created by millions of years of nature at work fascinated him. He went there several times and once told Ellie that when he died he wanted to be cremated and his ashes released over the canyon from a helicopter. Eleanor might well have given him his wish were it not for her fear of flying. In fact, on one visit to the canyon, Spencer wanted her to accompany him on a helicopter ride over the canyon but she refused. He went by himself and, upon returning, told her how he almost fell out in the process of leaning to get a better look. His wallet in his shirt pocket did slip out, falling helplessly into the canyon.

Returning from the canyon trip, Doc and Ellie were only a few miles from home when, near Ringtown, he ran a stop sign. Sure enough, the local constable saw the violation and pulled him over. As usual his first request was for the doc's driver's license. When Spencer told him he'd lost it in a helicopter ride over the Grand Canyon, Eleanor could not contain herself. With the two of them laughing, the poor man did not know whether to believe him or not. Regardless, he knew who Dr. Spencer was and let him go. Two months later, Dr. Spencer received his wallet intact via the U.S. Mail. It seems a backpacker on the canyon floor came across the wallet and kindly returned it to him.

Visits to foreign lands were part of the Spencer itinerary as well. Robert had been to Canada many times to hunt and fish. Lake Louise in the Canadian Rockies was one of his favorite spots. To the south, Eleanor remembered the California freeways that led to Tijuana since she was driving and the traffic was "horrendous."

Sometime during his first marriage, Dr. and Mrs. Spencer took a delayed honeymoon trip to Central Europe and Russia.* Jule shopped while Robert toured the great clinics of Europe, learning all he could. A revolutionary atmosphere took hold in Russia at the time of their visit, causing most things to be shut down. Robert

---

*It is my suspicion that this first trip was paid for by Jule's parents perhaps as a honeymoon gift for the one that they never properly took.

Dr. Spencer on Fifth Avenue in New York City. (Courtesy Atty. Harry Strouse)

was disappointed but learned enough in Germany alone to make the trip worthwhile. It was in Germany that he met Dr. Ferdinand Sauerbruch who later became Surgeon General under Adolf Hitler. On this same trip, Spencer met with Dr. Robert Barany in Sweden. Dr. Barany was a Nobel Prize winner in medicine. This European trip also included visits to Spitsbergen, Iceland, Norway, Denmark, France, Italy, Finland, and England. In later years Spencer made a second trip to Russia.

Robert Spencer could boast that on one trip he stood at the Arctic Circle only miles from the North Pole. He could brag as well that he had climbed the Andes. He once made a trip to Peru to witness the world's first nerve-block operation. Afterward he could not resist seeing firsthand the famous Andes Mountains of South America.

Another sojourn took him to Cuba. Steve Sukunda accompanied the doctor on this trip and remembered many of the details. The purpose of the trip was to meet Spencer's understudy, Dr. Elias, to see if he could learn anything from the young doctor.

As usually happened in the vicinity of Dr. Spencer, a curious thing occurred during the flight. A request was broadcast over the intercom asking if there was a doctor on board. Dr. Spencer responded and was led to a woman at the rear of the plane who had gone into labor. A short time later, Spencer presented her with a brand-new, healthy baby boy. When he returned to his seat Spencer told Steve the story. Steve slapped his thighs and laughed in that high-pitched manner that I can still hear.

One of the other passengers on the plane was a nurse from New York. Both she and Dr. Spencer ended up staying at the same hotel in Havana. Dr. Spencer noticed that she was showing a keen interest in Steve. He told Steve so and encouraged his assistant to see what she wanted. Steve told me she took him to a casino to have some fun. Steve recalled pointing out to her that nobody was winning money at the roulette wheel and other games. He was reluctant, as usual, to place any bets. The woman chided him for being a poor sport and suggested they go to dinner. They ate a meal of steak and returned to the hotel. The woman suggested a walk along the beach, but Steve said he'd better return to his room. Out of options, the woman flatly invited Steve to her room. For whatever reason, Steve insisted that he declined the offer and returned to the doctor. Steve told me that after they returned to the States, he would occasionally get letters from the woman, inviting him to visit her, but he never responded.

When it came to domestic trips of the urban variety, Dr. Spencer's favorite haunt was none other than the Big Apple. He loved spending New Year's Eve there. He came to New York at other times as well to see the Broadway shows and go out to dinner. Usually he and Ellie stayed at the Plaza Hotel where they had a standing offer for a room of which the tab was picked up by some very wealthy and prominent family from the Hamptons. It seems they owed him a favor.

Eleanor recalled how he liked to get to the city by late morning. After they checked in he would immediately drag her out to see two or even three movies right in a row before dinner. Then it was out again in the evening for a Broadway show. She said he ran around like a maniac when in the city and she could barely keep up with him. She also said they moved around the city without fear, for the diminutive doctor had friends everywhere, thanks to the favors he had performed for so many people who lived in the city.

Over the years the gratitude shown to the doctor by so many people was considerable. Eleanor ran through a partial list for me. There were books by the hundreds. In fact, several years after his death, she gave over six hundred books (these were the ones she didn't want) to the library. He received cameras (which always delighted him), blankets (many of them handmade), linens for the bed (she told me she had enough of these to last a lifetime), candy, baskets of fruit, hand-loomed carpets, exotic foods, witty sayings to hang on the walls, shirts, ties, cuff links, tie clasps—at this point I stopped her.

Wherever they went, the doctor sought out the unusual. Flea circuses and sideshows delighted him. Once he took Eleanor into a sideshow at the Bloomsburg Fair, a huge agricultural fair held at Bloomsburg, Pennsylvania, every September. Inside, the man inserted a needle that the doctor himself examined into his vein. Then he proceeded to fill the tube in the needle with blood on command. Next, he emptied the blood back into his vein by sheer will alone. The entire trip home, Eleanor recalled, Dr. Spencer talked about how he had never seen anything like it. It annoyed him immensely that he couldn't scientifically figure out how the man managed to pull off such a stunt.

Robert Spencer never missed an opportunity to check out the contents of any nearby gun shop. Weapons of destruction were always something of interest to him as he was an excellent marksman in his own right. Museums were also near the top of his list of things to see. It didn't matter if they were botanical, zoological, natural science, or historical. If there was one there he had to go through it.

Like so many highly intelligent people, Spencer's interests were varied and prolific. In addition to all his other interests, Robert was an amateur astronomer. He had thousands of dollars' worth of equipment and could spend hours at night charting the heavens. Many times he bought such toys without the slightest idea of how he was going to pay for them. Robert was also a student of geology and a gemologist. His collection of fossils was superb. No matter where he went, he brought back rock and fossil samples of the area. He also collected gems and had his own equipment to cut and polish them. He learned jewelry making so he could make use of his gems.

As we already know he did his own animal taxidermy as well as preserving and mounting the plant and insect specimens displayed throughout his home and office. He was a master photographer, sometimes building his own cameras and developing his own prints. He appreciated fine art and food as well. He was partial to seafood in particular and enjoyed such dishes as octopus, snails, frog's legs, whale meat, and tarpon. Once, on an impulse, he purchased an amphibious car. The strange-looking vehicle could be driven on the road or taken right from the road into a lake or river and used as a boat. Eleanor said it was one of his all-time prized playthings.

Consider for a moment this partial list of books that I noticed in his study: *Abortion*, *The Erotic Revolution*, *Chemotherapy*, *The Rock Hunter's Field Manual*, *The Philosophy of Nietzsche*, *A Handbook of Clock Repairs*, *History of Witchcraft*, *Protestant-Catholic Marriages*, *Birth Control*, *Nuclear Physics*, *A Woman's Guide to Man-Hunting*, *Poems for the John*, *Creative Glass Blowing*, *The Death of Adolf Hitler*, *Mark Twain's Letters from the Earth*, *Guide to Wyoming Wilderness*, and so on. This list of titles is a reflection of Dr. Spencer's range of interests, his love of the outdoors, and his sense of humor.

While discussing Dr. Spencer's many interests I would be remiss if I did not mention his passionate love for a good healthy debate with another intelligent person. The topic didn't matter as long as the participants had verifiable data to back up their points of view. He would debate with anyone anytime he could find an opponent. One of his beloved debating partners was Dr. Romualdo Schicatano, the same doctor who had saved Steve's hand.

Both Schicatano and Spencer were faithful members of the local Rotary Club. Spencer did not drink or socialize much (When would he have found the time?) and wasn't one who felt the over-powering need to bond with male companions. The once-a-week dinner meeting of the Rotary was one of the few social pleasures he allowed himself. Friends as well as foes, he and Schicatano often got into it, disrupting the dinner meeting. Schicatano may have been the only member of the local medical association who would be caught dead with Dr. Spencer. Sometimes they literally had to be separated. The other doctors in rural conservative Schuylkill County did not share Spencer's radical views. Also, they spurned him because he did not socialize with them, often interpreting this as arrogance.

A Rotary member once recounted to me one debate in partic-ular that he remembered vividly. The debate was about abortion and this time Schicatano started it.

"Bob, I don't care what you say. Both as a Catholic and a doctor I say abortion is immoral and wrong!"

"As a Catholic I can understand that but as a doctor I think you're being a hypocrite."

"I can't for the life of me see how."

"Well, as a Catholic you are blinded by the absurd taboos of your church. That's your excuse there. But, as a doctor I can't see how you can ignore the benefits of legalized abortion."

"It's immoral. That's how!"

"Morals are nothing more than what the majority say they are."

"And that's why it's immoral. The majority feels that way."

"Like hell! Over one million women a year have abortions. Do you call that a minority? Are one million women's lives so unim-portant that you can just dismiss them as a minority?"

"I think you know me better than that."

"Then it has to be because of your religion."

"Of course my religion affects my attitude. That's a given. But, that's a life you are destroying when you commit an abortion. I don't care what religion we're talking about."

"That's where you're wrong, my friend."

"How so?"

"Look, in the sixteenth century the great Roman Catholic Church didn't consider a fetus to be alive for the first forty to eighty days after conception. During that time period abortion wasn't even punished. It was okay. Then they changed their mind like changing a tire on a car, saying that from the moment of conception a fetus is alive."

"The Church was simply trying to set up more exacting guidelines for its people."

"If they truly believe that life begins at conception, then why aren't they lobbying to date the age of a child from conception instead of birth on the certificate?"

"Why? Because the fetus isn't actually existing in the outside world. It's still part of its mother."

"Exactly. It's not yet a part of the outside living world. Therefore it doesn't really exist yet. So how can they call it murder?"

"They can because the fetus is alive. You've heard the heartbeats of hundreds of them. You know they're alive."

"They are no more alive than the woman's appendix and they can be removed every bit as safely as any appendix you've ever taken out."

"Maybe so, but that doesn't alter the fact that it's still murder."

"It's only murder in the view of the Catholic Church. The Catholics, who are a minority in this country if you want to talk about minorities, are imposing their moral judgments on the rest of this country. Do you call that fair?"

"The Church isn't forcing its view on our legislators. It's just lobbying on behalf of its views and then let the lawmakers come to their own decisions."

"All right. By the same token, if the laws do change and abortion becomes legal, and that day is coming, Catholics won't be forced to have abortions. They will still be free to do as they please. Or, should I say, as the Church tells them to do."

"But the Church is afraid that such a change will lead to more promiscuity and a lowering of morals."

"So they try, through fear tactics, to make their parishioners tow the line. Morality can't be instilled in people through fear. It has to come from within. The tactics of the Catholic Church are as outdated as the Church itself."

"The Church is founded on doctrine and it's only trying to do the best it can within that framework. It can't just throw its basic doctrine out the window."

"Oh, but it can. And as sure as I'm standing here, some day in the future your pope will respond to that mysterious 'Divine Revelation' and issue a decree that changes the belief on abortion just as he will on birth control. Until then, he's forcing millions of women to suffer needlessly."

At this point the two combatants were separated and a feeble attempt was made to get on with the meeting. Despite it all their friendship would endure. It probably bothered Schicatano more than Spencer. Dr. Spencer was one man who learned early on in life that, in order to lead the orchestra, one has to turn his back on the audience.

If a friend in time of need is a friend indeed, then Robert Spencer had a true friend in Paul Reidler. Whenever the doctor needed him, he was there. Paul Reidler moved from Orwigsburg, a small town at the southern end of Schuylkill County, to Ashland about the same time Steve Sukunda did. In fact, he moved into the same boardinghouse as Steve and they became friends. When Paul's father became ill, Steve's advice brought Mr. Reidler to Dr. Spencer. Over time they became lifelong friends.

Mr. Reidler is ninety-one years young at this writing. Evidently he guards his close relationship with Spencer very protectively, refusing to speak with me about the man. Back in 1970 he was a little more talkative than now and I recall our conversation.

When Paul Reidler moved to Ashland he was young and poor. The furthest thing from his mind was a philosophy of life. Paul eventually got into the garment industry. He started a factory that made children's underwear. Soon it became very successful and he branched into other ventures. He made himself a millionaire several times over.

He told me that when he was younger he was too busy making money to even think about life and things like why we are here. As the money accumulated, he began to consider such thoughts. Whether he was influenced by Spencer is unclear, and he never said. He did say that he became, like Spencer, a freethinker and had the same basic life philosophy as the doctor.

Through the years, as has been mentioned, Dr. Spencer encountered financial problems. Paul was always just a phone call away. When Spencer got arrested, the bail money was assured. If lawyers' fees were a problem, Paul could be counted on. If the doctor purchased some expensive new equipment and was having difficulty making payments, he had Paul. They were soul mates as well as friends and it is doubtful Dr. Spencer would have survived some of his tough times if it were not for his solid friendship with Paul Reidler.

Dr. Spencer and Paul Reidler shared the same philosophy of life as well as social circles (that is, when the doctor could find time to socialize). Paul Reidler was financially sound whereas Dr. Spencer often found himself in financial difficulty. It was because of Reidler's emotional as well as monetary support that the doctor was able to get through those difficulties. Whenever Dr. Spencer needed him Paul was, like a true friend, there for him.

Chapter 10

FIGHTING THE LAW SPENCER-STYLE

How can I even give you words of gratitude when they seem weak beside your unconcern for gratitude. I can only try to give to someone else the understanding you have given me.

—thankful patient

Many readers are familiar with the saying "Justice delayed is justice denied." If so, you may have mixed feelings about Dr. Spencer's experiences with the legal authorities. Arrested three times and brought to trial twice, the doctor never spent a day in jail. Some will view this as one of the greatest travesties of justice in this country. Others will contend, the law notwithstanding, that the man deserved a medal and that it was truly Providence that justice was blind. I suspect that the passionate feelings of both sides are in direct proportion to their stance on abortion. Before you decide, allow me to chronicle Spencer's running afoul of the law.

Late in 1953, Dr. Spencer, at the woman's pleading, performed an abortion on one Lillian Frie of Pottsville, Pennsylvania. Several days after the abortion the woman's husband called Spencer. He demanded several thousand dollars from Spencer or he would go to the police and expose the illegal abortion. After lambasting him with expletives, Dr. Spencer hung up. He thought the matter was put to rest. It wasn't.

This was not Robert Spencer's initiation to the blackmail game.

It had happened before, several years earlier. A man from Spencer's hometown of Williamsport tried to shake him down. He received the following letter.

Dr. Spencer,

The D.A.'s office in Pottsville would sure like to get some witnesses who would testify against you. I know a fellow here in Williamsport who brought girls to you for illegal services. By giving the authorities in Pottsville the names of the fellow and the girls they can subpoena them to testify. To prevent this I advise you to bring 150 genuine $100 bills—no new ones please—to the road side rear on top of the mountain on Rt. 15 south of Williamsport. Go to the men's rest room outside of the screening around the side and you will find a stone with an X on it. Under this will be a can, place money in the can, replace the stone, and get the hell back to Ashland. I have a letter written, addressed, and stamped ready to send to the officials in Pottsville if you cross me up.

Have the money there by April 25. Tell no one. Do not return or have the place watched. You have plenty of money and are inheriting a fortune so I am told. Take a trip then after you have done this. I shall forget it then.

Dr. Spencer contacted the police and cooperated with them as they set up a sting operation. The man was taken into custody. He was charged, stood trial, and was found guilty.

Four days before Christmas on December 21, 1953, Dr. Spencer was charged by Lewis D. Buono, Chief County Detective in the city of Pottsville. The accusation read: "Dr. Robert D. Spencer of 531 Center Street, Ashland, Schuylkill County, Pennsylvania, did unlawfully with intent to procure a miscarriage of a certain Mrs. Lillian Frie of Pottsville, Schuylkill County, Pennsylvania, a woman then big, pregnant, and with child, administer certain drugs or other substances plus certain instruments upon her the said Mrs. Lillian Frie and did thereby willfully and unlawfully commit an abortion upon and procure the miscarriage of the said

Mrs. Lillian Frie and contrary to the act of assembly in such case made and provided."

Eleanor remembered how upset the doctor was after coming home from the courthouse. He couldn't understand how a woman he had helped could do such a thing only a few days before Christmas. His disbelief was short-lived, she said, for in a few days he was his old self and ready to fight to the end.

On January 4, 1954, a warrant was issued for the arrest of Dr. Spencer, but he was not served until January 6. Bail was set at $5,000 which the doctor immediately put up in cash. He was accompanied at this bail hearing by an Amy T. McCormick. I have been unable to determine who she was and why she was there.*

On February 13, 1954, the grand jury sat and heard testimony regarding the charge of abortion against Dr. Spencer and he was bound over for trial. Robert Spencer pleaded not guilty to the charge.

Dr. Spencer hired J. Howard Stutzman as his attorney. He was also represented by another lawyer, Mr. Kilker. They collaborated well and planned his strategy. Stutzman knew the prosecution would hammer away on the abortion issue. He chose to ignore this completely in his defense of Spencer. Instead, he struck equally as hard on the establishment of blackmail.

Apparently he was successful. The trial occurred one year later and on January 12, 1955, the verdict was handed down. In the case of the *Commonwealth* v. *Dr. Robert D. Spencer* on the charge of abortion, the foreman of the jury, Alva B. Rogers, announced they found the defendant not guilty as charged. Case dismissed.

Winning the court case was just what the doctor needed. Throughout the ordeal Dr. Spencer's spirits were low. It seemed to him that all his work and all his efforts on behalf of the cause of women's freedom to decide their own fate had been in vain. Now

---

*I have tried to present as much information as possible about this trial. In trying to gather more information about the trial, I was informed by an attorney familiar with the case that the court records had been purged.

he felt vindicated even if the law remained unchanged. He found new determination to continue his fight against the laws on abortion. He sought out every avenue afforded him.

One of the first places Dr. Spencer tried to enlist new support was the local Rotary Club. Now at each meeting he could be heard trying to persuade the members that his ideas on changing the laws should be adopted in a resolution by the organization. He would argue his case over and over to them. Dr. Spencer was never able to win them over, but he never stopped trying.

When they wouldn't adopt a formal resolution he tried to get them to sign a petition to the governor asking for a repeal of the law. Many of the members were Catholic and vehemently opposed to this. Among the others, half of them felt the moral issue was just too hot to handle. The rest were using the club meetings as an excuse to escape from their spouses and feared a yes vote would rupture the group, causing it to disband completely, removing their only legitimate reason for getting out of the house once a week. Only Paul Reidler stood with the doctor on the issue.

From the middle of the 1950s until his death, Dr. Spencer did everything he could, except buying radio and television time, to further his cause. He continued to write letters to the governor as well as state and national legislators. He joined organizations such as the Association for the Study of Abortions which lists as one of its objectives: "To improve understanding of the abortion problem through public meetings and the use of mass media." He sent out literature to anyone who expressed an interest. He was waging a one-man battle, a battle he started in earnest in 1925. I seriously doubt that Dr. Spencer viewed himself as a national movement. He was too humble and too dedicated to the daily treatment of patients to see himself in that light. I'm sure, however, that he took every opportunity to make his opinions known and lend support to any cause that mirrored his own.

Dr. Spencer had less than one year to enjoy his legal victory and renewed attack on the establishment. On December 9, 1956, his world came crashing down. That day an abortion patient named Mary Davies died on his operating table.

Mary Davies lived in New York City. She was a part-time student at Columbia University and worked part-time at Irvington House, a children's treatment center for rheumatic fever. She was twenty-six years old, single, and pregnant. When she arrived in Ashland on December 8, she had a little over $160 in her purse and the other half of a return bus ticket which she would never use. What happened is described by Dr. Spencer himself in a written statement.

"At approximately 10 A.M. on December 9, 1956, Miss Mary Davies, [of] New York City, came to my office alone. She was also at my office December 8, 1956, about 3 P.M. On her December 8 visit she was alone and told me that she had been bleeding for the past two weeks. I did not examine her. I told her to come back to see me Sunday. I gave her pills for pain and ergotrate tablets to stop the bleeding. She left and returned [on the ninth], for the purpose [of receiving] a D and C. I put her to sleep with 13 ccs of evipal made into a solution to make it a 10 percent solution. I injected that solution into the vein of the left arm and in ten seconds she was asleep.

"The next I noticed, she was not breathing very well and her face appeared blue. I gave her 5 ccs metrozol into the muscle of her left leg. When I saw that she did not respond, I gave her an injection of 5 ccs in the vein. When this did not work, I started artificial respiration and used my oxygen tank, placing a tube into her throat. When that failed, I gave her an injection of adrenaline. One injection into the vein and two injections into the left breast. I tried more artificial respiration and pulled on her tongue, but got no response. I worked on her a full hour and did all I could think of, but she expired about 11:30 A.M.

"The assistant, Mildred Zettlemoyer, was called in to help me give artificial respiration. Then I went for adrenaline in my laboratory in another office on the first floor. I had my assistant, Mrs. Zettlemoyer, call Steve Sukunda, Walnut St., Ashland, who is employed by me as a laboratory technician and works every day but Sunday. I was going to go into air passages in the trachea. This would give light to see into the trachea. However, the battery was dead. I could not use this. When Steve arrived I told him it was too late, that the patient had expired. When the patient expired, I placed the body in another room and took care of my other patients. . . . I believe that this patient died in my office from some heart disease."

Eleanor told me she would never forget that Sunday night when Douglas returned home from the clinic. He had not called her for fear of upsetting her. She said she took one look at him when he came into the room and said, "Something terrible happened today, didn't it?" He told her about the woman's death. She remembered that not once in their conversation did he express any concern for himself personally. His sole interest was that a woman had lost her life and he didn't understand why.

After Mary Davies's death, Dr. Spencer called the county coroner's office to report the incident. He, in turn, called the district attorney. That same day a charge was drawn up for abortion against the doctor. On February 21, a warrant was issued for his arrest. The bail hearing took place on March 1 with bail being set at $10,000. Thanks to Paul Reidler the bail was made. In the March term of 1957, the grand jury again found a true bill and ordered Spencer to stand trial for illegal abortion; unexplicably the charge of manslaughter was dropped. Spencer would suffer the uncertainty of the outcome for almost two years before getting his day in court. Despite this, Eleanor reported that the people continued to come to him and Dr. Spencer continued to serve them in the same manner as he always had. It was as if the whole thing never happened.

Dr. Spencer rehired the duo of Stutzman and Kilker to represent him. He also retained a third lawyer by the name of Walter Sidoriak as a consultant. Spencer was wise in the political ways of Schuylkill County and the addition of Sidoriak to the team proves it. Walter Sidoriak was self-centered, egotistical, and presumptuous. The right stuff for a lawyer in a seemingly hopeless situation. Walter Sidoriak was a very prominent Catholic in the community of Minersville—a brash move in having such a well-known Catholic as a member of your defense team. Walter was also married to the sister of Judge James Curran who would be presiding over the trial. This fact alone should have excluded Curran from serving in this trial, but, this was Schuylkill County. Walter Winchell, the famous national columnist, is reported to have said in one of his articles that "If you want to commit murder and get away with it, Schuylkill County is the place to go."

Oddly, I knew Walter Sidoriak personally. I lived across the street from him for about twenty years. I caddied for him at the Schuylkill Country Club when I was a teenager. He had the most unorthodox swing I ever saw but he could hit the ball a country mile. He had this bizarre habit of walking around with his jacket half off his one shoulder like a bewildered street person. He fancied himself a singer and took voice lessons in New York. On the golf course I would be subjected to his operatic singing in Lithuanian as we walked the fairways to his next shot. Three doors up the street from his home was a barroom that he frequented. My good friend's father owned the bar and my friend and I hung out there. I can still see Walter coming into the bar in the late afternoon and plopping himself down on a stool. He would look at the bartender and yell "Caw! Caw!" This was the signal to give him a shot of Old Crow Whiskey. He would down two or three of these then put his money on the bar and leave without uttering a word to anyone.

Confident that our solid relationship would open doors for me, I crossed the street one day in 1970 to interview Walter Sidoriak. I rang the bell. Walter opened it about six inches and merely looked at me. I told him I wanted to ask him some questions about the Dr. Spencer case that he took part in. He slammed the door shut in my face without ever speaking a word. Perhaps I should have persisted but I was inexperienced in such matters and totally stunned. In retrospect, I shouldn't have been. He was a strange fellow.

Headlining the list of cases to be heard in the Schuylkill County Criminal Court in January of 1959 was *Commonwealth v. Dr. Robert D. Spencer* on the charge of performing an illegal abortion. At last the two sides were ready to do battle.

January 7, while gathering the pool of jurors from which the twelve would be selected, an unexpected setback was dealt the defense. A recess was called because of a mysterious illness befalling Judge Curran. In addition, attorney Stutzman was unavailable because he was tied up with a case in superior court. Also, several New York doctors scheduled to appear were unable to come, further complicating matters.

District Attorney Robert Harris turned over the prosecution to lesser well known and experienced Assistant D.A.s David Bechtel and Calvin Friedberg. This boded well for the defense. Judge C. M. Palmer replaced Judge Curran as the presiding judge for the trial. This move must have worried Walter Sidoriak and the rest of the team.

On January 9, jury selection got underway. Of the 150 people called to do their duty only ninety reported. The arduous task of picking the right ones (for both sides) began. Dr. Spencer not only participated in this with his lawyers, but his input was critical in getting the desired mix of jurors who would be sympathetic to his case. I read the notes he wrote and passed to the team as each juror was being considered. If he wanted one passed over he would write "fixed opinion." For another that he wanted he wrote "wife of patient" (which should have disqualified her). Another he favored he wrote "worked at colliery" knowing full well his favorable reputation among the miners.

By lunchtime only three jurors had been picked: Arthur Weaver of New Boston (the foreman), William Yodis of Shenandoah, and Pauline Willier of Pitman. At this point the D.A.s had used up three of their eight challenges. The defense, one. This was the same day that the manslaughter charge was "held in abeyance" by the prosecution. The reason given was that the manslaughter charge was a misdemeanor with a one-to-three-year sentence while the abortion charge was a felony bringing with it a ten-year sentence. The D.A. wanted to concentrate on the heavy stuff.*

Sidoriak and the team were smiling. Not only was there one lesser charge to defend against but they would use this to their advantage, telling the jury that the prosecution didn't even care about the woman's life. They would say that obviously it didn't matter to the prosecution whether she lived or died. Their only concern was trying to besmirch the reputation of the only man who tried to help her.

By the end of the next day, January 8, fifty-six jurors had been called and examined by the five lawyers. Of these called, three were disqualified for having served in the past year; eight were thrown out by the Commonwealth; seven were challenged by the defense; and twenty-six were excused for having fixed opinions as to guilt or innocence. Two alternates were selected in case some misfortune befell those serving. The twelve chosen were:

Arthur Weaver, laborer from Morea (foreman)
William Yodis, laborer from Shenandoah
Pauline Willier, housewife from Pitman
Joseph Dabrilla, unemployed from Frackville
Mrs. Wally Sears, housewife from Jonestown
Stanley Mashock, policeman from McAdoo
Lulu Anns, housewife from Minersville
Betty Scheitrum, housewife from West Penn
Raymond Michael, retired from Pottsville
Catherine Chappell, housewife from Gilberton
John Tracey, laborer from Minersville
Hayden Evans, contractor from Tamaqua

---

*Also, if the jury had two charges to decide, they could always go for the lesser one. If only one charge is offered, those who vote guilty have to vote for the more severe charge or let him go free.

The seven-man, five-woman panel was duly sworn in. Not a single one was from Ashland. Mr. Bechtel addressed the jury first. He told them that the Commonwealth would prove an abortion was performed on the deceased pregnant woman, which was contrary to the law, despite Dr. Spencer's statement that such a procedure was imperative to the woman's physical condition. Bechtel went on to say that the prosecution would prove that the woman came to Ashland by bus from New York City on December 8 and Spencer gave her pills in preparation for a D and C, asking her to return the next day, whereupon he put her on the operating table where she succumbed while having an abortion. He took the time to mention that although the woman died at 11:30 A.M., the doctor did not call anyone, but placed her body in another room while he attended to other patients. When he did call someone it was 3:00 P.M. and the call was to his attorney. Bechtel emphasized that only after consulting with his attorney did Spencer contact the authorities. Later that day an autopsy was performed. Bechtel promised that the results of the postmortem would prove that the operation was not imperative and that the act was illegal.

At the end of the day, Judge Palmer called for a one-day recess since Mr. Stutzman was to appear the next day in supreme court to argue a case. On January 10 the trial resumed. Dr. Spencer's statement was read in full to the jury. As an addendum to the statement, Dr. Spencer added that he called Kilker at 1:00 P.M. and the lawyer did not arrive until 3:00 P.M. at which point he (Spencer) immediately called the coroner's office.

Chief County Detective William Keuch took the stand and testified that he received a call from the coroner and went straight to Ashland to investigate. He examined the woman's room at the Hotel Loeper and was present during the autopsy performed by Dr. Emmit Hobbs. Afterward he took a bottle of unidentified pills and some vital organs to New York City where he turned them over to Dr. Milton Helfern and Dr. Alexander Goettler; the latter being a toxicologist and the official New York City doctor.

COURT HOUSE NEWS

By AL DIETZ

Woman Died in Dr. Spencer Office Of Anesthesia, Expert Testifies

Dr. Milton Helfern, specialist in pathology and chief medical examiner for New York City, testified yesterday afternoon that it was his opinion that Mary K. Davies died of evipal (sleeping drug) poisoning, which was administered as the anesthesia during an operation.

His testimony was given in the trial of Dr. Robert D. Spencer, Ashland, who is charged with performing an abortion and abortion resulting in the death of Mary K. Davies, of New York. The girl died in Dr. Spencer's office on December 9, 1956.

Dr. Helfern testified organs from the deceased girl were brought to his office in New York City by Chief County Detective William Keuch on December 11, 1956, for examination.

He testified that his findings from the examination of the organs showed that pregnancy existed and that pregnancy was

Lindbergh Witness

Dr. Alexander Goettler, New York City, toxologist, who testified yesterday in the trial of Dr. Robert D. Spencer, at the Court House, is the same toxologist who testified in the Lindbergh kidnaping case in the early 1930's.

removed by an operation just prior to her death.

Dr.. Helfern testified he found no abnormalities in the organs except for congestion. He also testified that in his opinion he did not think the operation was needed.

Dr. Alexander Goettler, of New York City, toxocologist, testified he made an analysis of the organs brought by Detective Keuch and found evidence of 13.3 grains of evipal sodium in the girl's body. He testified that the quantity of evipal was a significant quantity;

also that it is used for administering anesthesia.

Local Doctor Testifies

Dr. Eula Eno, Pottsville, testified this morning that it was her belief that Mary K. Davies died from poisoning by anesthesia, administered to her for the purpose of doing a D and C operation, which would result in an abortion.

She also testified it was her belief that the girl was not in need of a therapeutic abortion. She explained to the jury the meaning of a therapeutic abortion. She said it was performed when a patient's life is in imminent danger by the continuation of pregnancy, then the pregnancy is interrupted.

Dr. Eno further testified that a therapeutic abortion is never done without consultation of another doctor. She also said that a D and C operation is universally performed in a hospital, under standard and medical practices, and not in a physician's office.

Local coverage of the Spencer trial in the Pottsville Republican *newspaper.*
(Author's collection)

Following Keuch, the prosecution brought on Dr. Otto Miller, the Schuylkill County coroner. He told how Spencer contacted him and how he and Spencer examined the contents of the woman's handbag to verify her identity. Here they found a bottle of pills from a New York drugstore. The pills had no doctor's name or identification of the pills on the label. Miller mentioned that he observed blood on the woman's lips and teeth but saw no abrasions or cuts to explain them.

The defense team cross-examined him. Dr. Miller admitted that a D and C, although an uncommon occurrence, was a medically acceptable practice under the proper circumstances. He acknowledged that there could be various women's disorders that warrant the procedure and that excessive bleeding could be one of them. He added that medication could be used to control it and that if necessary, the procedure should be done in a hospital. The defense did not discredit Miller; at best they only managed to soften the blow of Dr. Miller's testimony.

The afternoon brought a quick succession of uneventful testimony from the peripheral players in the drama. Ashland policeman Arthur Destreich testified that he was present when Officer Keuch secured the statement from Spencer and witnessed the signature. Under cross-examination he could not remember whether Dr. Spencer read the statement before signing it. A small token for the defense. Ashland undertaker Ray Madden told of being called to Spencer's office at about 4:00 P.M. on the day in question at which time he took the body to his morgue. He took a picture of her and conveyed her to the Locust Mountain Hospital for an autopsy by Dr. Hobbs.

The night clerk at the Hotel Loeper, Vincent O'Hearn, related the events when the woman checked in. He felt she looked perfectly normal and remembered seeing her later that night at dinner. Next came Mildred Zettlemoyer, Spencer's office assistant. She testified that she sterilized instruments for the doctor and on that day she came into the operating room at his request and aided him in giving artificial respiration until the woman expired. The trial was off to an excellent start from the prosecution's point of view.

If the winter day of January 14 was dark and cold outside, up on the "hill" it must have been even worse inside the courtroom. There were some real heavyweights scheduled to sit in the chair and take the oath. The first was Dr. Milton Helfern, Chief Pathologist and Medical Examiner for the City of New York. On deck was Dr. Alexander Goettler, the same nationally renowned toxicologist who testified in the infamous Charles Lindbergh kidnapping case in the 1930s. The prosecution wanted to win this case badly.

Dr. Helfern stated that, in his opinion, Mary Davies died of evipal poisoning which was given to her as the anesthesia for an operation. He further stated that he examined the woman's organs brought to him by Detective Keuch and that these tests showed her to be pregnant and that this pregnancy was terminated just prior to her death. He went on to observe that he found no abnormalities in the organs except for congestion. He also stated that he did not think the operation was needed. Helfern was fresh off his recent triumphant appearance as an expert witness in the famous Sanders "Air Bubble" case in which a New England doctor caused the death of a female patient.

Dr. Alexander Goettler took the stand next. He testified that his analysis of Davies's organs found evidence of a significant quantity of evipal sodium in the body and that was the cause of death. He described in detail the "melting test" used to measure the amount of drugs found in vital organs. He also testified that a D and C was performed on her for the express purpose of terminating her pregnancy. Dr. Spencer's attorneys did not ask a single question of either of these two damaging witnesses! "No Cross" was their reply to Judge Palmer.

Dr. Eula Eno, a gynecologist and obstetrician from Pottsville, was hired by the prosecution as a consultant for this case. She was next on the stand. She stated her belief that Mary Davies died from anesthesia poisoning given to her for the purpose of an abortion. She added that the woman did not need a therapeutic abortion, going on to explain to the jury that one of these is performed only when the woman's life is in danger. It is always done in a hospital and never without the consultation of at least one other doctor. Her testimony was just as damaging as that given by the two eminent physicians who preceded her. Again, the defense did not cross-examine.

Dr. Emmit Hobbs followed Dr. Eno on the stand. He became the fifth physician to declare the cause of death to be the drug administered as the anesthesia. He reiterated all of the previous opinions regarding evidence of an abortion, no reason for its being done, and so on. This time Stutzman took the coroner to task in cross-examination. He was able to get Hobbs to admit that the current tests used to determine pregnancy were not always 100 percent accurate. It was the high point of a low day for the defense trio and their client.

January 15 was a crucial day for the trial. Dr. Arthur W. Ludwig, the New York City physician and a specialist in internal medicine who treated Mary Davies, was called by the prosecution. Dr. Ludwig testified that he first treated Miss Davies on March 9, 1956, for a problem with her menstrual cycle which caused cramps, bloating, and weight increase. He prescribed a low-salt diet and gave her two prescriptions: one for the evacuation of fluid; the other a barbiturate to act as a mild sedative. He said he treated her again on April 9 and May 6. Ludwig saw her again on October 26 when she was one week late for her period but could not find any evidence of pregnancy. Dr. Ludwig saw Mary Davies for the last time on November 1, whereupon he took a urine sample to determine if she was pregnant. When the prosecution asked the results of the test, Stutzman objected. His grounds were that since Ludwig did not personally examine the specimen, he could not answer the question. The objection was allowed, preventing Ludwig from answering.

Mr. Stutzman proceeded to cross-examine Dr. Ludwig. Under cross, Ludwig identified the medicines he had prescribed and was forced to admit that he could not identify the other pills found in her handbag. He was asked by Stutzman if any of these pills might induce an abortion but could not offer an opinion.

Finally, the prosecution called a local pathologist, Dr. Joseph Leskin, to the stand. At this point, Judge Palmer must have been growing impatient. He called both prosecution and defense lawyers to the bench and a discussion ensued regarding what the appearance of yet a seventh doctor was going to add to the case. Apparently the prosecution agreed and Leskin was excused without testifying.

Then, to everyone's surprise, the Commonwealth abruptly announced it rested its case. A startled attorney Stutzman asked for a short adjournment citing the unexpected occurrence and explained that his witnesses were not present in court. The judge announced a break and both camps scurried to their respected conference rooms.

One can only conjecture what took place as Stutzman, Kilker, Sidoriak, and Spencer huddled together in that room. The action they took suggests one of two schools of thought. Either they felt the ship was going down and there was nothing to do except start planning an appeal, or they knew something that nobody else knew.

When court came back in session, Mr. Stutzman made an equally surprising declaration. He was ready to make his final statement to the jury. He would call no witnesses. He would not put Dr. Spencer on the stand to defend himself. He would offer not a shred of evidence of his own.

Mr. Stutzman approached the jury with confidence, being careful not to appear arrogant. Then he began a closing that took no more than ten minutes. He observed that the Commonwealth had failed to disprove one word of Dr. Spencer's original statement. They had not shown that the injection of evipal was excessive or illegal. He also reminded them that it had not been proven that any of Spencer's instruments had been the cause of death.

He took time to emphasize the state-of-the-art facilities of Spencer's clinic, listing a fully equipped operating room, X-ray machine, on-site darkroom to develop and interpret films, a diathermy room,* a separate arthritis room devoted solely for the treatment of that ailment, and an elaborate laboratory capable of running tests on almost every kind of blood, tissue, and cells. Some of these items, he noted, were not even found in many hospitals.

Next, he went after the big-city doctors. He struck hard at Ludwig who, he reminded the jury, was Mary Davies's own per-

---

*A room where therapy was applied to the body tissues via high-frequency electromagnetic waves.

sonal physician. He recalled for them that Ludwig admitted not prescribing many of the pills found in her possession, some of which were barbiturates. He made reference to Helfern as the world-renowned authority on sudden and violent deaths, impressing on the jury that Helfern had not told them that an abortion caused the woman's death. He finished up with Goettler. Stutzman said the eminent toxicologist never testified that Dr. Spencer administered a lethal dose of any drug to Mary Davies. More importantly, he pointed out that neither the prosecution nor Goettler performed an analysis of all of the over fifty assorted pills found in the deceased's purse, some of which might produce an abortion or even death.

Mr. Stutzman concluded by saying directly to the jury that no hard physical evidence was ever produced to show that Mary Davies was pregnant or that any operation was ever performed by Dr. Spencer to abort the presumed pregnancy. Opinions don't matter; evidence does, he would say. If the jury could not say with certainty that Davies was pregnant, then they could not convict on a charge of abortion. Stutzman told them it was clear and simple what they must find. The defense rested.

Stutzman finished his short, eloquent speech at approximately 1:30 in the afternoon. By 1:45 the jury left the courtroom to deliberate and the vigil began. The prosecution, after the testimony of some of the most prominent physicians in the country, must have been optimistic. Apprehensive best characterizes how the defense must have felt. Neither side would be held in suspense for very long.

The jury deliberated a total of four hours and forty-five minutes, including time to have their dinner. They returned to a packed courtroom at 7:15 P.M. and announced their stunning verdict. Not Guilty!

What went wrong from the prosecution's point of view? They seemingly had everything they needed to get a conviction yet failed to do so. Perhaps my interviews with some of the jurors will shed some light. As any good lawyer will tell you, picking the jury is probably the most important and difficult part of a trial attorney's job. Evidence and witnesses notwithstanding, a jury is made up of complex human beings. When the trial is over they retire to a separate room where the drama plays itself to the tune of hang-ups, prejudices, and sometimes just the plain desire to get the darned thing over with and go home. It is as difficult to predict as the next stock market crash.

My interview with Mrs. Lulu Anns was very revealing. The Protestant housewife from Minersville noted that the jury members were all older, married people, somewhat sympathetic to a young woman's plight. It could very well have been their own daughter. She knew Dr. Spencer but said nothing about this when being selected. She had a chronic skin condition on her legs and found Spencer's homemade salve the only relief for it. She told me she must have bought a hundred jars of it over the years. She would send her money by mail and the boxes of salve would be mailed to her home.

It was her opinion (and that of most of the jurors) that Mary Davies tried, through some inept person, to have an abortion before she came to Ashland. The "bad job" wasn't working and out of desperation she went to Dr. Spencer who was merely trying to help. She took the trial seriously, recalling how she could not sleep or eat during the days of the trial. Lulu remembered Dr. Spencer thanking each one of them personally after the verdict. Later, Walter Sidoriak took them all out to dinner and saw them home. Lulu gave me one parting comment. She said she thought the New York doctors "were a bunch of snobs!"

Mrs. Wally Sears was the Catholic housewife from Jonestown on the jury. She said that Dr. Spencer, with his bow tie and gray hair, came off as a father figure, certainly not a murderer. He was a kind old man who she was convinced would not hurt anyone intentionally. Although Catholic, she felt abortion was a much better alternative than a woman committing suicide out of desper-

A copy of the official trial verdict. (Courtesy Schuylkill County Courts)

ation. If done by a competent doctor, she had no objection. She even restored to memory the courthouse dinner menu: "Delicious homemade bread with baked beans and cold cuts."

Mrs. Sears told me how the first vote taken was 11—not guilty, 1— guilty. The lone holdout was John Tracey from Minersville. He was somewhat embarrassed to find himself alone with his guilty vote. A second vote reaped the same result. On the third vote, seeing that the others were obstinate and anxious to get home, Mr. Tracey threw in with the opposition and the deal was done. Dr. Spencer was "not guilty."

Out of desperation, the district attorney's office again invoked the charge of involuntary manslaughter on May 14, 1959. It was dropped a short time later when the realization set in that a conviction was unlikely.

To investigate Dr. Spencer's third run-in with the law we must move forward to late 1965. Although it was business as usual at the Spencer Clinic the doctor was slowing up. In his mid-seventies now, failing health was taking its toll. He was no longer able to do

nd Daily

PA., FRIDAY, JANUARY 16, 1959

Dr. R. D. Spencer Acquitted by Jury On Both Charges

Dr. R. D. Spencer, of Ashland, was acquitted on both charges against him in county court at Pottsville growing out of the death in his office of Mary K. Davies, of New York City.

The jury got the case late yesterday afternoon after Dr. Spencer's counsel, J. Howard Stutzman, abruptly ended the trial when he produced no witnesses on the stand and in his address to the jury contended the Commonwealth had failed to prove its charges of abortion and death by abortion.

Atty. Stutzman also pointed out that the Commonwealth had failed to break down the original statement of what had happened as presented at the trial's outset by Dr. Spencer.

The jury was out four hours and forty-five minutes and at 7:15 o'clock last evening came in to Judge C. M. Palmer, the trial judge, with the verdict of not guilty on either count.

Atty. Stutzman had informed the court at the close of Wednesday's session that he would require "about 10 minutes" to present his defense to the jury, saying that the Commonwealth had not produced any evidence to show that the injection of a barbituate, used by the doctor in preparation for the operation, was in excess amount or, that the drug had been injected illegally.

The jury was also told by Stutzman that the Commonwealth had failed to present any evidence to show that any instrument used in

(Continued on Page Six)

Dr. R. D. Spencer Acquitted by Jury

(Continued from Page One)

the operation had induced an abortion or had been the cause of death.

Much emphasis was placed by Stutzman on the facilities in Dr. Spencer's office, which included an X-ray machine, a darkroom for the interpretation of X-rays, a diathermy room, an arthritis room for the treatment of that ailment; and a laboratory for the examination of blood, tissue and cells, utilities not found in the office of every practicing physician.

Stutzman also directed the attention of the jury to the evidence presented by the girl's own physician, who testified that the girl was under his care for a menstrual disorder from early in January 1956 to December 1956, with certain types of drugs prescribed for her, some of which were found among the fifty assorted pills the girl was carrying with her when she died.

Stutzman struck hard at the evidence presented by the girl's physician, Dr. Arthur W. Ludwig, of New York City, who testified that he had not prescribed all of the medicine carried by the girl, some of it being in the "barbituate family" of drugs.

Reference was made to the testimony given by Dr. Milton Helpurn, New York City medical examiner and world renown-

ed authority on sudden and violent deaths, in that Helpurn had not indicated to the jury that an abortion had caused the death of the girl.

Stutzman struck, too, at the testimony of Dr. Alex Gettler, New York City toxicologist, whom he said failed to testify that a lethal dose of drug had been administered by Dr. Spencer, and for the failure of the Commonwealth to have an adequate analysis of all of the medicines in the girl's possession to determine if any could have induced abortion.

Stutzman concluded his address by pointing out that no positive facts were introduced to show that a pregnancy existed or that an operation was performed to induce abortion.

Shoe Specials

Women's and growing girls' flats and heels reduced more than 50%.

GALLAGHER'S

21 N. Oak St.   Mount Carmel

NOTICE

Amvets Auxiliary, District No. 7, will meet at the Gordon Amvets No. 44 for the Installation of Officers Sunday, January 18 at 2:30 o'clock. Buffet Luncheon Will Be Served.

(Signed)

HELEN GETTY

Ashland Daily account of the trial verdict. (Author's collection) ten abortions a day plus minister to a full day's slate of regular patients. Time was running out and he knew it.

It was around this time that the more serious of the accidents to Steve Sukunda occurred. The story was in the local newspaper and one man read it with more than a passing interest. The man knew all about Dr. Spencer, having referred numerous women to the clinic for Spencer's specialized services. Like a divine revelation the man was struck with an idea that was pregnant with possibilities. Enter Harry Mace.

Harry Mace was a used-car salesman from nearby Williamstown, Pennsylvania. As I recall, Williamstown was known for being the hometown of the all-pro, football tight-end Gary Collins of the then Cleveland Browns. Everybody in town knew Gary and everybody in town knew Harry.

Harry Mace sold used cars but, as more than one person told me, you always saw the same cars on his lot year after year. I knew only one person who bought a car from Harry. It was a Lincoln Continental sedan and within a few weeks the transmission went on it. It was obvious that Harry's means of making money allegedly lay somewhere beyond the confines of the car lot.

Allegedly, and I say this because to my knowledge, like Dr. Spencer, Harry never did jail time. That is where the comparison between the two men ends. If there was any illegal activity going on in the west end of Schuylkill County, Harry was thought by many to have his hands in it. The mainstay of his operation was reported to be a brothel located at the exotically named Trade Winds Bar and Hotel.

At six feet tall, weighing over three hundred pounds, and with his dark-brown hair, Harry Mace was an Oliver Hardy look-alike. He was blessed with the gift of gab and knew how to use it to his full advantage. This large, robust man was both charming and disarming. So charming was he that once Harry relieved the government right out of one million dollars in a small business loan to build a new hotel and bar. He named it the Fountain Blue. His new home was attached to it. Unable to gain access to the records, it's a safe bet that the government never recouped any of the million. Ironically, Harry lost his versatile vocals to a bout with throat cancer. In his latter years he was relegated to speaking with much difficulty in a guttural, raspy voice.

And so it was that Harry Mace, pseudobusinessman and orating innkeeper, approached Dr. Robert Spencer. Harry proceeded to attack the doctor's Achilles' heel: his total conviction to the business of abortion. He told the doctor that he agreed completely with the effort to legalize abortions. Saying it should have happened years ago, he offered to help. He said he knew that Steve's accident had left the doctor shorthanded, giving sympathetic attention to how difficult it must be to find oneself in such a situation.

Harry proposed an efficient way to be of service. He would field the requests from women. Then, he would personally get them to the clinic and return them when they were finished. Harry would even collect the money from these customers, freeing the good doctor for more pressing matters. The doctor, so he said, would only have to concentrate on being a doctor. He even devised a plan to contact his many influential friends and start a campaign to raise funds to build Dr. Spencer a brand-new clinic to carry out his work. Unfortunately, it was a ruse, and worse, it worked.

Dr. Spencer foolishly welcomed Harry to the fold. It proved to be a mistake. Harry kept part of his promise. He was handling the women and bringing them to Spencer. A man in his position came across many such women needing the doctor's care. Business picked up at a time when Dr. Spencer was least able to accommodate it. The doctor's fee for an abortion around this time was one hundred dollars. Harry told them it was six hundred and kept the other five hundred for himself. Steve claims neither he nor the doctor had any idea what was going on.

Eleanor said the "Harry Mace Period," as she referred to it, was one of the darkest, most sordid chapters of Dr. Spencer's medical career. "It never should have happened," she said sadly. Harry was bringing in large numbers of women and young girls. The scene at the clinic became too busy and too open, she recalled. It got sloppy in ways that Douglas would never have allowed in his earlier years. Harry was bringing the women in and charging them for it—hundreds of dollars. The more women he recruited, the more money he made.

Harry got so caught up in the easy-money scam that he was bringing in more women than the doctor could handle. In addition, Harry was hustling the women out sooner than they should have been so he could make room for more to maximize profits. The patients had undergone a general anesthesia. By moving them out too quickly, some were collapsing on the street outside the clinic. The townspeople were getting upset and Eleanor was very worried.

She recollected one day in particular when Harry brought a woman to the doctor. She was a particularly difficult case and required a lot of Douglas's attention. This didn't stop Harry from bringing more and more women in. Things began to back up. Cars were parked haphazardly all over the main street and people were beginning to spill out of the clinic onto the street. The scene was chaotic and dangerous.

It was during this time, Eleanor said, that the doctor's already poor health took a serious downturn. His angina got worse. One day he came home to tell her he thought he was going to die that day. He said he lost count of how many nitroglycerin pills he had to take just to keep going. She scolded him and told him it was time to quit. She knew such advice would have no effect. He would ease up for a while, she would say. Then, a frantic mother would bring her pregnant fourteen-year-old daughter to him and before you knew it, he started right back up again.

The authorities were always watching Dr. Spencer but they couldn't believe what they were now seeing. Harry Mace was turning things into a circus. Something had to be done. This time Dr. Spencer would not get advance warning of what was coming.

The district attorney waited until he had what he considered a damaging airtight case and then he made his move. On February 23, 1966, at 3:45 P.M., Schuylkill County District Attorney Harry W. Lightstone and Assistant District Attorney Richard B. Russell stood before the honorable presiding judge James J. Curran in Courtroom No. 1 in Pottsville. The following is an exact transcript of what took place according to court records.

Mr. Russell: If the court please, I have at this time a request for the court to issue a search warrant to search the premises of Robert D. Spencer, M.D., at 531 Centre Street, Ashland, Pennsylvania. We have the affidavit here of the prosecutor of the case, presented today, to No. 286 March term, 1966, charging Robert D. Spencer M.D., Harry F. Mace, Michael Chickersky, and Steven Sukunda with abortion and conspiracy to do an unlawful act. The affidavit is sworn to by Corporal Charles Skurkis before the clerk of courts, and he is here to give additional testimony, if you so desire.

The Court: Very well. Put him on the stand.

Charles Skurkis, called on behalf of the Commonwealth, was duly sworn and testified as follows:
DIRECT EXAMINATION BY MR. RUSSELL:

Q. Identify yourself, sir.

A. I am Corporal Charles Skurkis, a member of the Pennsylvania State Police, stationed at the Mahanoy City barracks.

Q. And you are the prosecutor in this case, entered No. 286, March term, 1966, whereby Robert D. Spencer, Harry F. Mace, Michael Chickersky, and Steven Sukunda are charged with committing the crime of abortion and conspiracy to do an unlawful act. Is that right?

A. Yes sir.

Q. And upon whom was this alleged abortion committed, according to your information?

A. On Miss Lucille Carol Kingman, of Buffalo, New York.

Q. Buffalo, New York?

A. Yes sir.

Q. Will you tell the court briefly how you came into this information which has been alleged?

A. We received information on January 10 from the homicide division of the Buffalo, New York, Police Department that stated, in effect, they received a dying declaration from Lucille Kingman. It was taken by members of the homicide division, Buffalo, New York, Police Department, at the Millard-Fillmore Hospital, and that statement indicates that she had an abortion performed on her by Dr. Spencer, Harry F. Mace, Michael Chickersky, and Stephen Sukunda, at Doctor Spencer's clinic at 531 Centre Street, Ashland, Schuylkill County, on the 3rd, 4th, and 5th days of January of 1966. She stated $600.00 was paid to Harry Mace for this operation. She was treated daily.

Q. Is she still alive?

A. Yes, she is.

Q. Have you talked with her since the time of this original statement?

A. Yes, I spoke with her on three occasions.

Q. Has she given you a sworn statement?

A. Yes, she has given me, in company with the other police, sworn statements in addition to the dying declaration.

Q. To the same effect?

A. Yes.

Q. Did you get sworn statements from other persons?

A. Yes, from James Genco.

Q. Will you identify him; how he fits into this picture?

A. James Genco operated the automobile down from Buffalo on the 3rd day of January to bring Miss Kingman to Doctor Spencer's clinic.

Q. Who made the arrangements, for the abortion to be committed, with Doctor Spencer?

A. Doctor Spencer, James Genco.

Q. Who made the payment?

A. James Genco made the payment of $600.00 to Harry Mace.

Q. And this is from a sworn statement of James Genco?

A. Yes sir, a sworn statement in my possession.

Q. You are seeking under this affidavit for a search warrant to take the medical appointment books, the books of account, and other medical records of Dr. Spencer for additional evidence in support of the indictment? Is that right?

A. Yes sir.

Q. And that she appeared in his office how many days?

A. The 3rd, 4th, and 5th day of January 1966.

Q. And does your information indicate where the miscarriage actually happened?

A. Yes sir.

Q. Where was that?

A. At Doctor Spencer's office, 531 Centre Street. Ashland.

Q. Have you also . . . Did you receive any sworn statement from the doctor who treated Miss Kingman thereafter?

A. No sir. We spoke with the doctor at the hospital, Dr. Richard Romanowski, at the Millard-Fillmore Hospital.

Q. And did Doctor Romanowski indicate to you, according to his information and examination, that an abortion had been performed on this woman?

A. Yes sir.

Q. And the doctor told you as you testified today before the Grand Jury?

A. Yes sir.

The Court: Officer, it is your request that this search warrant be issued and that by the use of such warrant, you will be able to obtain the medical records, the account books, and so forth that were used as indicated from your conversation with the victim in this case.

A. Yes sir. She registered her name, too; and it was recorded in Doctor Spencer's record.

By Mr. Russell:

Q. Did she tell you how she registered?

A. Yes, under the maiden name Andrulizzi.

The Court: Very well. We are satisfied. The warrant may be issued.

Mr. Russell: If the court please, we also make a formal motion for the issuance of the capias for the arrest of these four men: Robert D. Spencer, Harry F. Mace, Michael Chickersky, and Stephen Sukunda.

The Court: On the basis of the fact that the indictment was found by the Grand Jury, naming the four men as defendants, as presented in the District Attorney's bill?

Mr. Russell: Yes.

The Court: The motion for the capias is allowed, and the court is granting the search warrant on the basis of the information presently presented before the court.

Mr. Russell: The officers are going to leave now to go to Ashland. Shall I remain in the courthouse?

The Court: Yes, and advise me. I will be here or will let you know where I am.

> (The hearing was recessed at 4:15 P.M.)
> (After recess)

The Court: We are ready gentlemen whenever you are.

Mr. Russell: If the court please, we have the four defendants in court in the case of Commonwealth versus Robert D. Spencer, Harry F. Mace, Michael Chickersky, and Stephen Sukunda entered to No. 286, March term, 1966. It is the purpose here that your honor would fix bail for these defendants. The charges are, as your honor may remember, abortion and conspiracy to do an unlawful act. Do you want the four of them to stand forward at one time or one by one?

The Court: Have you advised them of the returns of the Grand Jury and the indictment?

Mr. Russell: I understand that they all have been advised of that, that they are . . .

The Court: First, let us make sure of that.

Mr. Russell: First of all, Doctor Spencer, are you acquainted with the fact that the Grand Jury has found a true bill against you on the charge of abortion and the charge of conspiracy to do an unlawful act?

Doctor Spencer: Yes.

Mr. Russell then proceeded to ask the exact same question of each of the other three men. Each of them answered in the affirmative.

Mr. Russell: And were you, each of you, informed that you had the right to have counsel represent you? Doctor Spencer?

Doctor Spencer: Yes.

Mr. Russell repeated the same question to the others and got the same answer from all.

Mr. Russell: Did anyone of you want to have counsel here during this proceeding? First of all, Doctor Spencer?

Doctor Spencer: I have spoken to Mr. Stutzman.

Mr. Russell: Well, I spoke to Mr. Stutzman, and I will explain our conversation to the court. Now, Mr. Mace, did you want to have counsel represent you?

Mr. Mace: I called my lawyer and he told me just what takes place, and I have someone with me to go my bail.

Mr. Russell: Mr. Chickersky?

Mr. Chickersky: No.

Mr. Russell: You don't want to have a lawyer?

Mr. Chickersky: No.

Mr. Russell: Were you told you could have counsel represent you?

Mr. Chickersky: Yes, I was told.

Mr. Russell: Mr. Sukunda, did you want to have a lawyer here?

Mr. Sukunda: I don't understand.

Mr. Russell: This is a hearing to fix bail. Do you want your lawyer here?

Mr. Sukunda: I will have bail.

Mr. Russell: Would you like us to call someone?

Mr. Sukunda: Yes, Harry Strouse.*

Mr. Russell: Very well. We'll have someone try to reach him now. Your honor, I will say for the record that Harold Stutzman was called by Doctor Spencer, and I spoke to him on the phone; I told him this hearing was for the purpose of the setting of the bail, and he said all right, as long as he would have a proper bailman, and he asked what the amount of the bail was, and, at that time, I said I don't know; and I assume that the same will be with Mr. Strouse after we contact him.

The Court: Very well. Wait until Mr. Strouse is reached, and the defendant who asked for Mr. Strouse can go in and talk with him on the telephone.

(After recess)

Mr. Lightstone: Your honor, I spoke to Mr. Strouse and told him of Mr. Sukunda's request, and he told me to advise Mr. Sukunda if it is only for the purpose of this hearing for the fixing of bail, that he will not come down, but that he will be available to raise bail if bail is fixed. Do you understand, Mr. Sukunda?

Mr. Russell: The defendant said that is fine.

---

*Harry Strouse was an attorney living in Ashland at the time.

The Court: The court is directing that bail in the amount of $5,000.00 be furnished or fixed for each of the defendants in the several indictments that have been presented here.

Mr. Russell: Does the court mean that each defendant will have to post $10,000.00 or $5,000.00 total? There are two indictments, No. 286 and No. 286A, March term, 1966.

The Court: $5,000.00 for each of the defendants for both of the indictments, a total of $5,000.00 for each of the defendants.

Mr. Russell: If your honor please, should we list this as $2,500.00 for each indictment, or shall we . . .

The Court: Let me look at them. (He looked at the indictments.) Let it be modified. On the charge entered No. 286, March term, 1966, the amount of bail shall be $2,500.00 for each of the defendants, and on the charge No. 286A the amount shall be $2,500.00 for each. That would be a total of $5,000.00 for the two bills. Is there anything further?

Mr. Russell: That is all we have your honor.

The Court: Very well. Court stands adjourned.

When the state police raided the clinic that afternoon, one of them called Dr. Spencer aside and apologized for the intrusion. He told the doctor, "We are really after Harry Mace but I guess you're going to have to go down with him." Steve explained during our interview that shortly before the raid they found out about Harry's scam. One of the women came into the office madder than a wet hen, complaining that she was told the cost would be $100 but she had to give Harry Mace $600. Dr. Spencer was furious with Harry and just as unhappy with himself. How could he have been so gullible as to allow this to happen? he asked himself. Why didn't he see it coming?

All four of them almost spent the night in jail. The courthouse official who received bail and issued the okay for them to leave agreed to stay late. He felt he owed Dr. Spencer that much. He once had a nasty sinus infection that no one could seem to cure until he went to see Spencer. Since then he had been trouble-free. Dr. Spencer remembered and thanked him. Eventually, that night all four made bail. Dr. Spencer put up bail for Steve and Chickersky (who was a local handyman they had hired to help lift the women off the table and transfer them to the recovery room since they could no longer manage it alone). Once the word got out about the raid, several people arrived at the courthouse with enough cash to make bail. Paul Reidler was one of them.

For yet a third time Dr. Spencer found himself arrested and charged with performing an illegal abortion. It came at a time when his health was failing and he was seventy-seven years of age. Eleanor said that they wanted Harry Mace out of circulation so badly that, this time, it was felt a conviction of the doctor was almost certain. Even his lawyer feared the worst. In the end it really didn't matter. Dr. Spencer would cheat the prosecutor out of a conviction again. He would die before the case was brought to trial. The district attorney eventually dropped the charges against Mace, Steve Sukunda, and Michael Chickersky.

Chapter 11

WINTER OF DISCONTENT—
THE FINAL ANALYSIS

What you have done for me, I could never repay in words nor money. . . . There is such a deep fondness and gratitude that I feel. . . . I've learned so very much these past few days and I feel stronger in being and stronger in wisdom. . . . Thank you from the very bottom of my heart, and God bless you.

—grateful patient

Those of us old enough to have lived through the psychedelic sixties remember it as a period of turmoil and change unlike any time before it. Three years before the start of the decade the Soviets beat us into space with their *Sputnik*. It was as psychologically devastating as Pearl Harbor. A feverish race for space swept the country as Congress passed a bill to entice more college students into math and science to catch up with the Soviets.

The controversial Vietnam War began to rage, sparking controversy and protests nationwide. Only ninety miles from U.S. soil the Communist revolutionary Fidel Castro, who once had a tryout for professional baseball, seized power in Cuba. And who could forget the Cuban Missile Crisis? The 1960 Republican Convention in Chicago nominated Vice President Richard Nixon. The Democrats met in Los Angeles and chose John F. Kennedy. In the closest national election ever, Kennedy became the youngest and first Catholic president in history.

During the 1960s a new and inner-directed awareness of self emerged. Juvenile delinquency spread as the nation's population began to shift from the cities to the suburbs. Teen gangs knifed and brutally beat rival gangs. Pornography legally entered the U.S. mail for the first time as speech protected by the Constitution. Drug addiction and alcoholism reared their ugly heads as parents blamed the pervasive influence of television and comic books.

In spite of this dark picture, evangelist Reverend Billy Graham attracted the largest crowds ever to New York's Yankee Stadium. People were seeking answers. Credit cards proliferated for the first time. "Charge it and feel like a king" was the slogan of the decade. And, speaking of kings, Elvis Presley surged onto the American music scene becoming an instant icon.

This was the scene that greeted Dr. Robert Spencer during the last years of his life. It was vastly different from 1925 when he first opened his doors in the tiny town in Schuylkill County. Ashland had changed much over the years. The prosperity that coal brought years before had long since vanished. When coal was king most of the towns boasted twice their present populations. Then, money flowed freely and unemployment was rare. As the 1960s began the end of that era was in evidence all around. Businesses went under as money was tight. Deep, ugly, open-pit strip mines dotted the landscape and lay abandoned once the coal had been obtained. The hardy, virile miners who were used to making a living by the sweat of their brows were relegated to surviving, instead, by the sweat of their fraus. The men loafed idly on the streets as their wives found employment in the many garment factories that sprung up in the coal region. In places like those owned by Paul Reidler, they toiled in harsh conditions for the lowest of wages.

Through it all, the doors of Dr. Spencer's Center Street clinic remained open. The clinic was one of the few going concerns in town, even if he was far from amassing a personal fortune. The hard times made it even more difficult for him to ask for money from his patients.

Late in the 1960s, it was a source of great disappointment to the doctor, now in the autumn of his years, to realize that the nation's

A serious Dr. Spencer in the autumn of his years. (Courtesy Atty. Harry Strouse)

abortion laws were still unchanged. There were rumblings but, they were small consolation to him. In January of 1967, the *New York Times* ran an article on Gov. Nelson Rockefeller's call for a revision of the eighty-four-year-old New York abortion law. He urged that abortion be permitted when the physical or mental health of either the mother or the child were endangered; he also sought the right to an abortion if the pregnancy were due to incest or rape. The Catholic community vigorously opposed the move and a Right to Life Committee was formed to fight the proposal.

The *Times* article also stated that same year a National Opinion Research Center Poll found that a majority of Americans (including Catholics) backed more liberal abortion laws. Sixty-four percent of Catholic men and 58 percent of Catholic women favored this move. It is reported that in Czechoslovakia, over 140,000 abortions were performed without a single fatality.

According to a March 1967 *New York Times* article, in March of

1967 a setback was dealt to the pro-abortion camp. The New Jersey Supreme Court ruled against the parents of a child born defective due to German measles. The Glietmans tried to bring suit against their doctors for not telling them their child would be defective and for not performing an abortion. The court decided against them, citing a defective child's right to life is greater than the parent's desire for an abortion.

By April of 1967, Colorado Governor John A. Love signed into law a new abortion bill, perhaps the nation's most liberal. He feared his state would become a mecca for abortions. A year later Governor Rockefeller still found himself lobbying for a revision of the New York law. He urged people to keep in mind that abortion was a legal and medical problem, not a religious or political one. He proposed a committee of ten distinguished persons to study the issue.

A National Opinion Research Center Poll reported in June 1968 that 40 percent of unmarried students were having sex. Of those who got pregnant, 80 percent had abortions. Law or no law, people were finding ways to get the abortions they desired. General Curtiss LeMay, the vice-presidential candidate of the American Independent Party, backed legal abortion.

Mentally and spiritually, despite having lived more than three-quarters of a century, Dr. Spencer's intellectual ability to withstand punishment was still intact. His physical condition was quite another story. The last two years of his life saw a substantial deterioration in his health that began to affect his mind. His blood pressure rose dangerously and he never left home without his heart pills. The angina pain was ever present. He had his nitro pills for that. Unknown to most around him, Spencer had detected symptoms of the onset of diabetes. He worried about this.

The doctor was also suffering from prostitis (enlarged prostate) as well as a double hernia. However, to him, the most serious problem he had was the dismal condition of his legs. The many years of standing and straining over the operating table had spawned an ugly case of arteriosclerosis. The debris-filled veins and arteries bulged from his legs like a road map. The pain it caused him was excruciating, greatly reducing his mobility.

Eleanor had to help him up and down the stairs for fear he would stumble. The walk each morning to the clinic took three times as long. The pain would force him to stop at every other parking meter for the strength to move on. Townspeople were familiar with the image of a bow-tied man whose gray hair protruded from under his beret. The doctor was often seen leaning on parking meters as he made his way to work.

Mrs. Spencer sadly told me how the farthest they could then go on vacation was to Atlantic City. They always stayed at the Chalfonte Hadden Hall Hotel. Where once he was always on the go, now Dr. Spencer sat in a wicker chair on the huge front porch of the hotel reading his medical journal. It troubled her greatly to see him in this situation.

On their last trip to Atlantic City the condition of his legs worsened and they had to cut short their stay. When they got home, Dr. Spencer was rushed to Geisinger Medical Center in Danville where Eleanor recalled he was confined to bed for days. He was given blood thinners, and a tent was set up over his feet and legs, pumping in warmed, highly oxygenated air. It took all their medical skill to save his legs from amputation.

The letters from desperate women kept coming in and Eleanor said she would answer them, telling the women that the doctor was unable to work. She recommended they go elsewhere to solve their problem. After his discharge the doctor returned to work as he valiantly tried to return to his usual schedule.

Financially, although not poor, Dr. Spencer's assets were meager given that he had spent almost half a century practicing medicine. Eleanor laughed with a trace of bitterness when rumors of her husband having secret bank accounts in Switzerland reached her ears. She showed me a stack of bounced checks over a foot high. The only time he even mentioned Switzerland was when he had once wanted to go there to see a world-famous surgeon who was having success replacing damaged veins with plastic ones in patients' legs. He never made the trip. He waited too long and was no longer in any condition to travel.

I once came across a financial statement of Dr. Spencer's for the year 1964. It listed total income for the year at $103,000. Expenses were not yet figured in. I was told by someone who was in a position to know that Spencer's net worth around that time was about $120,000. A good part of his wealth was money he inherited when his mother passed away. Actually, Steve Sukunda was probably worth more than Spencer. The story was given to me that Steve got into the stock market right around the time of the Crash of 1929. He invested in blue-chip stock and stuck with it over the decades. His reluctance to part with a buck was legendary and when he died in 1981 he left a considerable sum of money which went to distant relatives somewhere in Ohio.

Painfully, during the last two years of his life, Robert Spencer paused to reevaluate in an effort to find direction. The prospect of enduring a third court case was discouraging. His forty-year effort to change the laws on abortion with no concrete results was disheartening, and the realization that so many elements of society despised him for what he was doing was disquieting for him.

During our conversations Eleanor shocked me by saying that for a moment or two Douglas actually considered quitting the abortion business. He told her that if he did he would have wanted to specialize in rectal, urinary, and venereal diseases. He enjoyed these specialties more than any others. She said she almost believed him, but then a call would come in from a woman in need and he'd "be right back at it."

Despite feeling frustrated and suffering from major physical illness as well as depression, he would not be defeated. His basic optimism along with the persistent drive to adhere to the standards he long ago set for himself sustained him through this difficult introspective time. These were the most salient aspects of his personality and they helped him toward a stoic resignation to continue to do all that he could in the time that he had left. He knew there wasn't much.

In January of 1969, Eleanor had finally prevailed in getting Douglas to do something about his double hernia. He consented to an operation. The hernia condition actually was the result of an "occupational hazard." Over the years he had lifted thousands of women from the table and carried them down the hall to the recovery room. Tipping the scales at no more than one hundred and forty pounds, many of the women outweighed him. It was merely a matter of time before the constant strain on his stomach muscles resulted in a hernia.

Down to one hundred and five pounds, as a concession to Eleanor Dr. Spencer paid an unexpected visit to Dr. Schicatano. A surprised Schicatano asked him what brought the doctor to his office. Spencer told him he was keeping a promise to Eleanor. He had a hernia and wanted Schicatano to look at it. After a thorough examination they sat down to talk. According to Eleanor, this is what she learned from Douglas.

Schicatano: I suppose I won't be shocking you by telling you that your blood pressure is—

Spencer: (interrupting Schicatano) I'm quite aware of how high it is.

Schicatano: Are you taking anything for it?

Spencer didn't answer. He pulled the ever-present pills from a pocket and flashed them at Schicatano.

Schicatano: Bob, do you know exactly how bad your legs are?

Spencer: Yes, every morning when I try to walk to work.

Schicatano: Then why the hell don't you quit? You know the possible complications that can set in.

Spencer: Of course I do so there's no need to discuss it. What else?

Schicatano: Your heart. It's not good, Bob.

Spencer: Yeah, but it's not that bad. I'll make it through the operation.

Schicatano: What operation? Bob, exactly why did you come here? You didn't need me to tell you that you have a double and it could become strangulated.*

Spencer: All right. I want you to take care of it for me. I know that murder is a mortal sin in the eyes of the Catholic Church so I figure I stand the best chance of surviving with a good Catholic like you behind the knife. I don't trust the other witch doctors and they don't like me anyway.

Both men laughed. It was perfect timing for an icebreaker. Schicatano agreed to do the operation. He asked one thing of Spencer; that he go into the hospital for a few days before the operation so they could monitor his vital signs and control his medication. Schicatano wanted no surprises when he operated. Dr. Spencer agreed and did as he was asked. The consultation between the two ended with Schicatano joking that he hoped the pope did not get word of this or he'd be excommunicated.

Dr. Schicatano must have been apprehensive about performing this operation on Spencer. He had a seventy-nine-year-old patient with serious multiple medical problems, any one of which could end his life. Worse yet, his patient had been medicating himself. He knew objectivity was critical in good diagnosis and treatment. How can one possibly be objective about one's own body? At least

---

*Constricted so as to stop blood circulation.

for the time being Dr. Schicatano could neutralize this while Spencer was under his care.

Schicatano was a skilled surgeon. He would do his very best to help the man he considered a friend even if he did have mixed feelings about his practice. The operation took place and went as planned. The tears in the intestinal wall were repaired. Dr. Spencer was moved to recovery with good vital signs. Schicatano had to be breathing a sigh of relief.

A few days later, Dr. Spencer was in his room feeling fine and in a very positive mood. Steve was visiting him in the early evening and they chatted. The doctor was saying that in another day or two his stitches would come out and he would be going home. He was looking forward to it.

Without warning, Dr. Spencer began coughing. The coughing spell got worse and Spencer asked Steve to help him get to the bathroom. Steve placed his arm under his friend's arm and began walking him to the bathroom. When they got one step into the bathroom, Steve said Spencer slipped from his arms and slumped to the floor without ever making a sound. Steve said he was dead before even hitting the floor and laid there before him in a crumpled heap, the victim of a fatal blood clot.

The date was January 21, 1969. The man who, through his competence and conviction, was the major force in the quest to legalize abortion, was dead at the age of seventy-nine.

A man is considered lucky if, in his old age, he is able to witness the realization of the dreams of his youth. Given this criteria, Dr. Robert D. Spencer was not a lucky man. He died before achieving the one goal to which he devoted his entire existence—that of seeing a single significant change in the abortion laws. This was without question his greatest disappointment. Yet, to judge him as a failure would be unjust, regardless of your stance on abortion.

His open defiance of the law for nearly half a century must be interpreted by a country undergoing a major social and moral metamorphosis as having a considerable effect on its future. In the long run no forward movement on the abortion battlefield would be shaped without experiencing the influence of this one man.

It is always difficult to gauge the success or failure of a person who was never quite able to reach his ultimate goal. As a general practitioner, Dr. Spencer was a gifted individual whose personal sacrifices for his patients were limitless. As an abortionist he was, if nothing else, prodigious. He had a natural tendency toward rebellion and a dislike for procrastinating, a trait that was often mistaken for arrogance.

It is often thought that the character of a person, once formed, varies little. Most of us remain essentially unchanged throughout our lives. Dr. Spencer's most noteworthy characteristic had to be the consistency with which he practiced the values he articulated and fought to maintain for nearly five decades. Once he arrived at the formulation of his life's philosophy, he steadfastly refused to modify it even in the face of imminent disappointment. If he did fail it was because he was a man of theory in a world of practice whose institutions resisted the changes he proposed rather than because of his own limitations.

Throughout his life Dr. Spencer never lost his basic optimism that change would eventually come. Even at the end, when an illness made him feel like a juggler who suddenly realized he'd got too many bowling pins in the air, the hope for change was alive and well within him.

Spencer envisioned a workable framework of abortion, birth control, and a new look at marriage not unlike the manifesto of the present younger generation. The doctor felt that modern marriages were breaking down because of people's inability to recognize that men and women have natural instincts that lead them to polygamous relationships. He proposed a greater degree of sexual freedom within relationships. This, he felt, would allow people to satisfy these basic drives, permitting them to later settle into a more satisfying relationship with a permanent partner. There was nothing immoral in this idea to Dr. Spencer simply because he

THE NEW YORK TIMES THU

Dr. Robert Spencer, 79, Is Dead; Said He Did 100,000 Abortions

1/2 3/69   Special to The New York Times

ASHLAND, Pa., Jan. 21—Dr. Robert Douglas Spencer, a physician who, by his own admission, performed more than 100,000 illegal abortions in this small played-out coal mining community, died Tuesday at the age of 79.

Not Reticent About Himself

By MICHAEL T. KAUFMAN

Dr. Spencer never believed in euphemisms. He was an abortionist and he called himself one. But he was far different from the popular stereotype. He operated openly from his 11-room clinic on Centre Street in the middle of Ashland, a town of some 12,000 ringed by the slag-heap sores of open pit mines.

Unlike those who perform abortions in makeshift quarters at odd hours for fees ranging up to $1,000, Dr. Spencer operated in antiseptic surroundings and said that he never charged more than $100. On the campuses of East Coast colleges he was sometimes referred to as "the angel of Ashland."

Last winter, while sitting in his study rimmed with books, the small, frail doctor explained how he gained that reputation. "I always figured a doctor is supposed to help people, to help the living," he said.

He went on to tell of his Methodist upbringing in Williamsport, Pa., where his father was once the district attorney of Lycoming County. He read Herbert Spencer, the English philosopher, became interested in science and took up medical studies at the University of Pennsylvania and at Jefferson Medical Center.

First Abortion in 1923

Then came a period of graduate study at the Rockefeller Institute. In the 1920's he moved to Ashland with his first wife, the former Julie Butler. He became chief pathologist at the Ashland State Hospital, a facility specializing in miner's diseases.

"In 1923 a woman came to me from someplace around here," the doctor recalled. "She was a miner's wife and she said he didn't want to have the child she was carrying and asked me if I could do something for her." That was his first abortion. He thought he charged her $5.

"As time went on my reputation sort of spread. I never made any attempt to hide what I was doing," he said.

Dr. Spencer spoke out at every forum for abortion reform. "Prohibition couldn't work, so how do they think they can legislate the sex instinct?" he commented.

He was a vocal and avowed atheist and frequently scandalized the weekly meetings of Ashland's Rotary, to which he belonged and of which he was fiercely proud.

Dr. Spencer maintained his regular medical practice as well, having left the hospital in the early thirties and opened his own clinic. He gained the support of the powerful United Mine Workers Union because of his willingness to go down into mines to aid injured miners. In 1934, he decided to go to the Soviet Union to study abortions, which he understood were being performed on a widespread basis. "When I got there, though, Stalin had gone into a puritanical stage and had outlawed them, so I never got to see one."

Since the thirties, huge bundles of mail arrived daily in Ashland, sometimes addressed only to "Spencer" or just "Doctor." These contained secretively worded requests for appointments. They came from as far away as California, England and France.

Acquitted in 1956

The doctor was arrested three times and was brought to trial twice. The most serious case occurred in December of 1956, when a young teacher from New York died on his operating table. He called the police and told the state trooper that the girl had died from a freakish reaction to sodium pentathol while he was performing an abortion.

In his trial in Pottsville, the Schuylkill County seat, his statement was read to the court. The defense presented no witnesses. A jury of seven men and five women then deliberated for four hours before returning a verdict of not guilty to the charge of performing an abortion.

Several years later an employe of the county administrator's office was asked how this could have happened. "There aren't too many people in this county he hasn't helped," he replied.

Dr. Spencer leaves a son and a daughter by his first marriage, which ended in divorce. In 1946 he married Irene Eleanor Becker, who survives.

(Author's collection)

found nothing immoral in the basic drives of the human body.

Dr. Spencer carried the unlikely mixture of hope and frustration with him all of his life. Success, in the larger sense as we all define it, appears to have eluded him to the end. It could be said about Dr. Spencer that someone like him walks among us but once in a lifetime. To some readers that will appear to be the best news in this book. To others it will be considered a true American tragedy.

Many articles appeared in print after Spencer's death. On January 23, 1969, in a special to the *New York Times*, the two-column headline read: "Dr. Robert Spencer, 79, is dead; said he did 100,000 abortions." The story began: "Ashland, Pa., Jan. 21—Dr. Robert Douglas Spencer, a physician who, by his own admission, performed more than 100,000 illegal abortions in this small played-out coal mining community, died Tuesday at the age of 79." The article, written by Michael T. Kaufman, went on to chronicle the life of Spencer—how he operated openly from his eleven-room clinic on the main street, never charged more than $100, his upbringing in Williamsport, his first abortion, trips to Europe to study abortion, his avowed atheism, the trial of 1956, and several quotes including how he got his reputation: "I always figured a doctor is supposed to help people, to help the living."

The February 17, 1969, *Newsweek* magazine ran an obituary for Dr. Spencer. Complete with pictures of both Spencer and his operating room, the article talked about the local miners' devotion to him, offered a quote from Steve Sukunda, and included reference to a study by Spencer presented to the Association for the Study of Abortion in Hot Springs, Arkansas, by a sociologist who had obtained the paper from Dr. Robert Spencer in their meeting the year before. The headline read: "King of the Abortionists."

The February 28, 1969, *Medical World News* reported on Spencer's first abortion in the early 1920s, and how he developed the paste he used to dilate the cervix and make the extraction of the fetus easier. It noted his graduation from the University of Pennsylvania Medical School in 1916, and how he interned at Philadelphia General and studied pathology at the Rockefeller Institute.

Time magazine of March 7, 1969, ran an article on Spencer entitled "King of the Abortionists." It reported that one year earlier, Great Britain passed a new abortion law that had turned London into the abortion capital of the world. Perhaps so, but only for the women with the money to get there.

The *Los Angeles Times* article of March 17, 1969, was by far the most impressive and comprehensive of the pieces written on Robert Spencer. Covering more than ten columns, the article gave an extensively detailed account of Spencer's life including the town of Ashland and his run-ins with the legal authorities. The item was written by Richard Dougherty and was well done, although there were some errors such as reporting Harry Mace as being from Tremont.

Dr. R. D. Spencer Dies at Ashland

1/22/69

DR. ROBERT D. SPENCER

Dr. Robert Douglas Spencer, 79, of 31 S. Ninth St., Ashland, for over 50 years, died at 5 p.m. Tuesday in Ashland Hospital where he was admitted Jan. 14. Born in Kansas City, Mo., March 16, 1889, he was a son of the late William and Emily Butler Spencer. When he was two years old, his family moved to Williamsport where his father was district attorney of Lycoming County.

A resident of Ashland for the past 50 years, Dr. Spencer was a 1911 graduate of Penn State College and a 1916 graduate of the University of Pennsylvania Medical School. Chief resident physician at Pottstown Hospital from 1916 to 1917, he served as First Lieutenant in the Medical Corps during World War I from 1917 to 1918.

Pathologist for Ashland Hospital from 1918 to 1925, Dr. Spencer opened his private practice in 1925, maintaining it until his death.

He was the first physician in Schuylkill County to use bronchoscopy, dealing with an instrument which may be passed through the trachea into the large bronchi and is used for removal of foreign bodies and diagnosis.

Dr. Spencer was a member of Ashland Rotary, Association for the Advancement of Science, Association of American Physicians and Surgeons and the National Geographic Society.

Surviving are his wife, the former Eleanor Becker, a former teacher in the Mt. Carmel Schools; two children, Louise, wife of Dr. Theodore Enterline, Philadelphia; William, La Jolla, Calif.; also three grandchildren.

Funeral services Friday at the convenience of the family from Frederick T. Kull Funeral Home, N. Ninth St., Ashland The Rev. Robert G. Hughes, of the Good Shepherd Chapel, will officiate; interment in Mt. Carmel Cemetery.

Obituary in the January 22, 1969, Pottsville Republican. *(Author's collection)*

Cavalier magazine published a story by Eleanor Aumont in August 1969. Entitled "Dr. Spencer Is Just Down the Street," it related her personal experience of going to Dr. Spencer for an abortion. The year was 1953 and she paid $40 for his services.

In June of 1998, *Playboy* magazine in its "Playboy Forum" section paid tribute to the memory of Dr. Spencer. Written by Paul Crasser, the article is titled "The Saintly Abortionist, One Man's Story." I quote the opening: "This year marks the 25th anniversary of *Roe* v. *Wade*, the U.S. Supreme Court decision that legalized abortion. It is an appropriate time to remember the late Dr. Robert Spencer." The article recounts how he started out doing abortions and how his reputation spread. Apparently Krassner became involved in referring women to Spencer; as many as several a day. He was subpoenaed before a grand jury but refused to give up Spencer's name.

In Schuylkill County, the *Pottsville Republican* ran Spencer's obituary on January 22, 1969, complete with a picture of the doctor sporting a bow tie. The headline read: "Dr. R. D. Spencer Dies at Ashland." The article goes on to mention all of the specifics of his life that have been previously told with one interesting exception. The word *abortion* is not mentioned once.

In a sense, Robert D. Spencer wrote his obituary some eight years before his death. He was asked to write up something to appear in a booklet for the fiftieth class reunion of his Pennsylvania State University graduating class. Here is what he wrote:

"Robert D. Spencer, M.D., 531 Center St., Ashland, Pennsylvania. The summer of 1911 spent at the Bureau of Animal Industry, Washington, D.C., in the Biochemical Division under Dr. Marion Dorset, who first made a solid media for growing the tubercular germ. In 1911–1912 taught biochemistry under Dr. G. G. Pond at the Pennsylvania State University. From 1912 to 1916 a student in the Medical School of the University of Pennsylvania; June to January 1917, an intern at the Pottstown Hospital, the only intern at the hospital at a time of typhoid epidemic; January 1917 to May

1918, intern at the Philadelphia General Hospital, taking the specialties including two months in the contagious hospital. This was at the time of an epidemic of meningitis and polio. When at Blockley I took the National Board Medical Examination and was the fiftieth one to pass this examination, General Gorgas having considerable to do with the organization of the board. May 1918 in the army; sent to the Rockefeller Institute, New York City, where I received intensive laboratory training, coming into contact with the top medical researchers in the country. July 1918, I was sent to the Army Medical School in Washington, D.C. About ten days later, I was placed in charge of Camp A.A. at Humphreys, Virginia. This gave me considerable experience with grippe, or influenza as it was termed. Discharged from the Army in April 1919, in 1920 I was the pathologist at the Ashland State Hospital. While I was at the hospital, I took a course under Dr. Chevalier Jackson, then associated with the University of Pennsylvania and became the first in bronchoscopic work in this region. In 1925 I left the hospital and started in general practice in Ashland.

"In 1934 I made a trip to many medical centers of Europe. In Munich, I met Dr. Sauerbruch, who later became Hitler's Surgeon General. In Sweden at the University of Upsala I met Dr. Robert Barany who was a Nobel Prize winner in medicine. The fall of 1934, I did the first prostate operation by the trans-urethra method done in this region, assisted by Dr. Green, one of the first in Philadelphia to do this operation.

"I have been in every state in the Union except the last one. In Alaska I shot one large moose and a black bear. I have been in Spitsbergen, Iceland, Norway, Denmark, Sweden, Germany, France, Italy, Finland, Russia, England, and many parts of Canada."

From a psychological point of view there are two things about this life summary by Dr. Spencer that I find intriguing. First, he never mentions either his first wife, Jule, or his second, Eleanor. Most of the other abstracts in the class reunion book said something about their spouses. Also, conspicuously absent is any mention of this lifelong quest—the legalization of abortion. I'm not sure what it indicates (perhaps nothing at all) but I would be interested in hearing an opinion from some experts who research such life summaries.

Dr. Spencer's funeral was held at the Fred Kull Funeral Home in Ashland. A minister from the Good Shepherd Chapel officiated. The doctor would have been amused at the scene, knowing his feelings about organized religion. The minister was Eleanor's idea. There were less than twenty-five people present at the ceremony. The only time I saw Steve Sukunda express any anger was when he described the funeral to me. "Where were all his friends? Where were all the people he helped over the years? And the Rotarians. Brother Rotarians. Where were they?" he asked with a downcast look.

Interment was in the Mt. Carmel Cemetery. The cemetery sits on a small hill looking down on the community of Mt. Carmel, Eleanor's hometown until she married the doctor. It would be more than a few years before she would join him there. Prior to his death, people from Greenwich Village in New York wanted to honor him with a trip to the city and a dinner in his honor. Ill health prevented him from attending. They sent him a check for $500 instead. Eleanor told me that at the time of his death, Robert was making plans for a trip around the world. She said she knew he would never make it.

Other than the local townspeople's memories there are but two pieces of evidence left in Ashland attesting to the existence of Dr. Spencer. The Dr. Robert Spencer Memorial Scholarship was started by Eleanor in memory of her husband. It goes each year to a local high school graduate planning to further his or her education in the medical field. The other, as of this writing, still stands at 531 Center Street. The stone-facade building sits abandoned; the numbers 531 barely visible on the faded white door. The empty lot next to it is overgrown with weeds.

A few days after the funeral, Eleanor was going through some of her husband's personal effects. She came across a medical diary that he began keeping when his health started to fail him. In it she discovered his description of the hernia operation as it was to be done by Dr. Schicatano. He had written down a list of all the possible complications that could arise. The last one on the list was embolism. It was the only one underlined and he had two question marks after it. Did Dr. Robert Spencer actually predict his own death? I, for one, am inclined to believe that he played the consummate diagnostician right up to the very end—his own.

For weeks after Dr. Spencer's death, hundreds of cards and letters of condolence poured in to his widow, Eleanor. I've picked one out to present here. There were probably more eloquent ones, however, this one caught my eye because it was one of the few that was from a man.

Feb. 1, 1969

Dear Mrs. Spencer,

I would first like to express my sincere sympathy at the loss of your husband. I read of his death in the *Village Voice* in New York and was deeply moved. Several years ago my wife had the extreme good fortune of coming in contact with Dr. Spencer. She told me of the kindness he exhibited toward her. I am writing to you to express my appreciation for all your husband has done not only for my wife but for all the others he has helped. If my wife had not been helped by Dr. Spencer when she was, her whole life would have been different and I am quite sure for the worse. I feel terrible at his loss.

I can only hope the laws under which we live can some day be changed to reflect the needs of the people in our society. He helped us when we were emotionally unable to raise a child. Thanks to him we now have a wonderful family life and two kids, twelve and seven. Although he is gone I want you to know that what he did for a young girl in her time of need will never be forgotten by me or her.

Signed,

An indebted husband

EPILOGUE

I am confident that enough evidence has been shown to establish two irrefutable facts in the medical career of Dr. Robert Douglas Spencer, a professional life that spanned from 1916 to 1969. First, he no doubt eased the suffering and saved the lives of many people with his expert practice of medicine. Second, without question and by his own admission, he was responsible for terminating thousands of pregnancies.

The medical community spurned him. Yet, they referred thousands of patients to him both for legitimate and illegitimate reasons. The locals held him in contempt, speaking his name in low whispers. However, they came to him in droves and protected him in his time of need. The citizens of the small town of Ashland, Pennsylvania, have not seen the likes of him since nor is it likely they ever will again.

Dr. Spencer never lived to see the fruition of his lifelong quest. The famous *Roe* v. *Wade* decision legalizing abortion did not come until 1973. Even then the muddy waters of abortion were not cleared. Opponents claimed the decision was too liberal and left abortion without controls. Advocates bemoaned that it still didn't erase all the restrictions and limitations.

The abortion debate is and will continue to be an emotionally charged issue. The Republicans traditionally take a tough stance against abortions while Democrats take a more liberal approach.

Both camps have their defectors. In 1992 the abortion debate became a key part of the presidential campaign, as it will into the foreseeable future. Bill Clinton came out in favor of choice. In contrast the Republicans, after much debate, stood fast on a pro-life platform. They even called for a constitutional amendment to ban all abortion.

Dr. Spencer claimed to be motivated by a great concern for the rapidly rising world population and a woman's right to govern her own body. In centuries past, population was held in check by famine, disease, and wars. Modern science has not eliminated these but it has made them ineffective as a means of population control. Today we have abortions, we have the pill, and we have the morning-after pill. We have vasectomies, tubal ligations, and condoms. In spite of it all our population grows.

Dr. Spencer would be fascinated (as he always was) by modern science. Genetic-engineering advances allow us to identify and correct defective genes, clone organisms, and make fertile a previously infertile woman. This is heady stuff but not without its ramifications. The controversy continues.

I leave it to you, the reader, to decide if Dr. Robert Douglas Spencer was a man of vision years ahead of his time; a true angel of Ashland. Or was he a disillusioned fanatic guilty of the most heinous of crimes?

INDEX